Improvising and Variations for Fingerstyle Blues Guitar

By
Pete Madsen

ISBN-13 978-0615946726

www.learnbluesguitarnow.com

Improvising and Variations for Fingerstyle Blues Guitar

By
Pete Madsen

Improvising and Variations for Fingerstyle Blues Guitar

By
Pete Madsen

Many early blues songs from players such as Robert Johnson, Big Bill Broonzy, Blind Blake and others were played using the basic "Cowboy" chords (chords played between the first three frets) that most beginning students have learned. Combining those chords with fingerstyle methods such as Travis picking (alternating bass) or dead thumb (monotonic bass) can be a joy in and of itself. But what if the student could take his/her knowledge of old blues tunes and learn to improvise with them? Using tools such as the CAGED system and using pentatonic scales we can open a new world of improvisation.

The key is being able to maintain a steady bass. We will show the student how to use chord voicings that maximize: 1) open strings and 2) fretted strings that are useful and powerful.

The CAGED system has become a part of the guitar teacher's vernacular. As a method for navigating the guitar neck it has a great deal of value for students who don't want to get bogged down in arcane theory. *Five simple chord shapes* provide the basis from which all guitar players (beginner, novice, advanced) can explore the guitar neck.

Most beginning guitar students are familiar with the first position chords: C-A-G-E-D. What many of them don't know is that they can apply these chord "shapes" to the entire fretboard to make any chord they want. Notice I use the word "shapes." It is essential that we shift our thinking from "this is a G chord" to "this is a G chord SHAPE." As we move that shape up and down the fretboard it becomes other chords.

As you work through the exercises and songs in this book you will notice that the different chord shapes lend themselves to experimentation and I encourage you come up with your own variations.

CHAPTER 1:
THE CAGED SYSTEM

In this chapter we will:

• *learn about the CAGED system*

• *learn CAGED shapes for major chords*

• *learn CAGED shapes for minor chords*

• *learn CAGED shapes for 7th chords*

• *strum through "Key to the Highway" and learn verse variations based on the CAGED system.*

CHAPTER 1
The CAGED SYSTEM

Those of you familiar with the first position chords, C-A-G-E-D, may not know it but you have at your disposal a powerful tool for navigating the entire fretboard. These simple chord shapes can be repeated throughout the neck to make chord inversions (same chord but with the notes arranged in a different order). Why is this valuable? Well, let's say we are playing a simple three chord song, e.g. CFG. You're playing the third verse and you are saying to yourself "I need to make this more interesting...up the drama." If you can move the same three chords up the neck the sound automatically becomes more interesting because the higher pitched notes give the impression of "movement" within the piece without overcomplicating things.

Part of the beauty of CAGED is that at its core it reduces the guitar down to 5 simple visual components: a C chord, an A chord, a G chord, an E chord and a D chord. From there we can expand outward to grasp as much of the complexity of the instrument as we wish. Most people are visually inclined and can lock into this system of chord shapes easier than say, having a teacher explain a lot of theory, which assumes a level of abstraction that may or may not be useful to the student.

Keep in mind: the CAGED system is a VISUAL system, but music is heard, not seen. The chord shapes are consistent in their relationship to each other, but the notes – the actual pitches we hear – will be different depending on where the shapes are played on the neck. A G chord, for example, is comprised of three notes: G-B-D. These notes can be found in various positions on the neck and on different strings. A G *SHAPE*, however, is visually what we are talking about when we look at a first position G chord. When we move that shape up the neck it becomes a different chord; if we move it up to the 5th fret, for example, it becomes an A chord: A-C#-E.

THE CAGED SKELETON

Example 1 lays out the bare bones skeleton of the system. You probably already know these chords: C-A-G-E-D. What you probably don't know is that you can work these chord SHAPES in this order up the neck to get higher pitched or lower pitched voicings of the chords. Notice I said *SHAPES* instead of actual chords. This is the major concept covered in this lesson: we need to shift our thinking from "this is a C chord" to "this is a C chord SHAPE" because we will be moving the different shapes up the neck to produce entirely different chords from what you might be used to.

FIVE DIFFERENT C CHORDS

In example 2, for instance, I have given you 5 different C chords: the first one is our normal C chord; the 2nd one a C chord with an *A shape*, the 3rd is a C chord with a *G shape,* fourth is a C chord with an *E shape* and finally a *D shape.* You should be able to see the shapes from the previous exercise but notice that there are often extra fingerings involved; this is due to the fact that we have to compensate for the lack of open strings. This can lead to some fingering conundrums – like the G shape. Don't worry, however, because there are some workarounds that make these chords a little more friendly as we shall see in exercise 3.

Before we go any further we should look at which notes make up a C chord. There are three notes: C – E – G. Even though we may be playing four, five or six strings we are actually only playing these three notes which can be repeated. For example in our first position C chord, starting from the 5th string, we are playing in order: C (5), E (4), G (3), C (2), E (1). Notice we play the C and E notes twice.

In the A *shape* C chord we are playing from the 4th string down: G (4), C (3), E (2), G (1). Same three notes but in a different order. The lowest pitched note in our original C chord is a C. The lowest pitched note in our A shape is a G. We are using the same notes but have *inverted* the order of the notes from low to high.

In example 3 we will play a C chord using a G shape. Notice I have written out three versions of this chord. The reason being is that the first version is not very practical, and I expect that many of you can't do the incredible finger stretch this requires. However, you can see that it ACTUALLY is a G shape. The next two versions of this chord strip away, one string at a time, the lower notes so that the third version is one you might find the most practical. It's still a bit of a stretch, but certainly easier than the first one. In fact, you can see that this looks a lot like the A shape we played in example two (the notes on the 4, 3 and 2nd strings are all played at the same fret). Only the first string is different: in the A shape you played a G at the 3rd fret; for the G shape you play a C at the 8th fret.

This brings me to another important point: we can use each shape within the CAGED system to connect to the next shape. This is important because when we start to form new chords we can find the next shape via the "connected" note, thus learning to navigate the fretboard! As we saw the G shape is connected to the A shape via the 4,3,2 and second strings. But how does the original C shape connect to the A shape? We need to add something to the C shape to form the connection.

In example 4 I am giving you a slightly different version of the original C shape. You would normally fret a C chord using your ring finger on the 5th string, middle finger on the 4th string and your index finger on the 2nd string. If you add your pinky to the first string at the 3rd fret you have added another G note: remember C-E-G are all part of a C chord. This G note at the third fret of the first string will connect you to the A shape of C. To get to the A shape from the C shape remove your fingers and place your index finger where your pinky was previously and place the other three fingers on the 4, 3, and 2nd strings at the 5th fret. For the G shape version of C we replace the three fingers that had been fretting the 5th fret with just the index finger barring and we can simply use the pinky to fret the first string at the 8th fret (the simplified version of the G shape). The pinky now provides the transition note for the E shape, which is a standard barre chord. Once again, the pinky in the E shape is the transition note as it becomes replaced by the first finger to form the lowest note in the D shape.

CAGED ex for improvisation

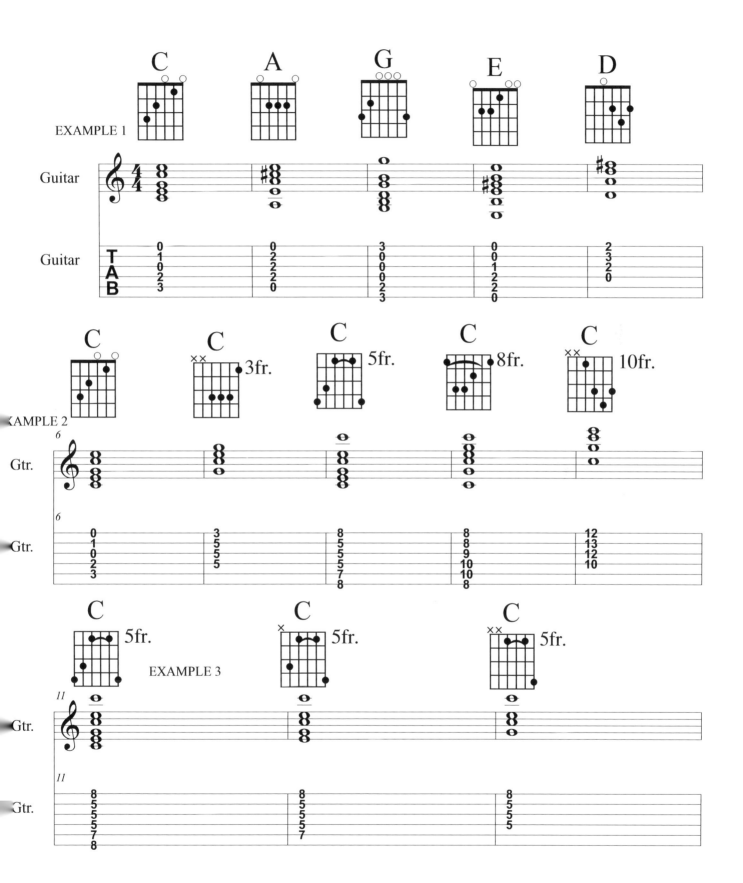

Example 4

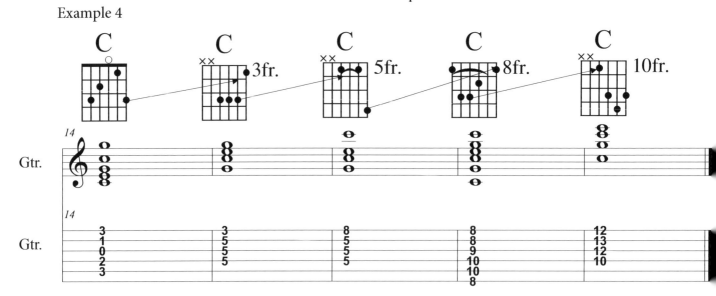

Gtr.

Gtr.

CAGED Minor chords

Now let's turn our attention to minor chords. Minor chords have a "darker" sound characterized by the root-minor third realtionship. Don't worry about what that means, just be sure you recognize the tonal difference between major and minor. You can use any adjectives you like to describe the difference, e.g. major=happy/uplifting, minor=dark/moody/brooding. Like the major chords most of these shapes should be familiar, but there are a couple that might seem a little strange. Most people know A, E and D minor but the C and G minor shapes are probably new to you. These particular shapes lack the finger freindlyness of most open position strumming chords and can be a little tough to fret.

They are probably better suited as arpeggios (chords played one string at a time), than as strummers.

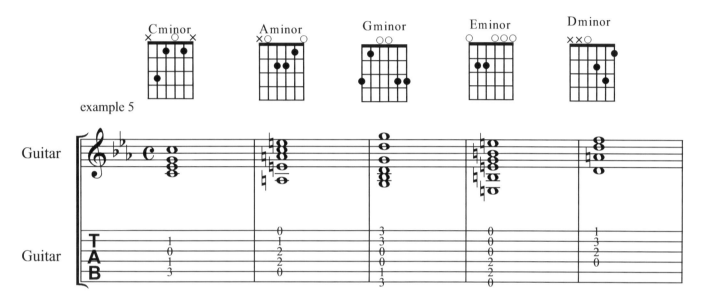

example 5

And here are the C minor chords with the CAGED shapes

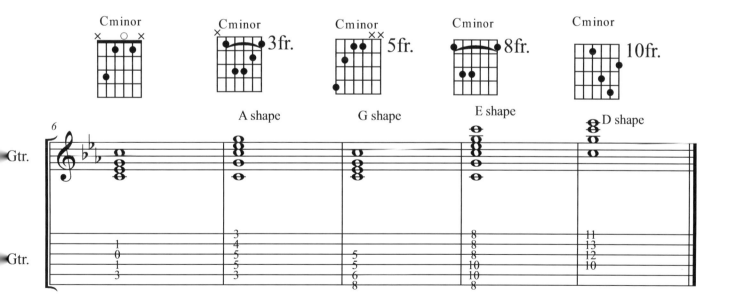

7

CAGED 7th Chords

7th chords

After major and minor triad the most important chords are dominant 7th chords. A dominant 7th is essentially a major triad with one note added – the flatted 7th from a major scale. 7th chords can be characterized as having a slightly unresolved sound, which makes them particularly useful in blues. Blues songs use a lot of 7th chords, so its important to know these shapes. Fortunately the CAGED forms of these 7th chords are probably already familiar to you. Example 6 lays out the standard C7 – A7 – G7 – E7 – D7 chords. In example 6a we create all C7 chords using the same shapes. These chords shouldn't be too difficult -- except for the G7, which like the original G chord provides some interesting challenges for our fingers.

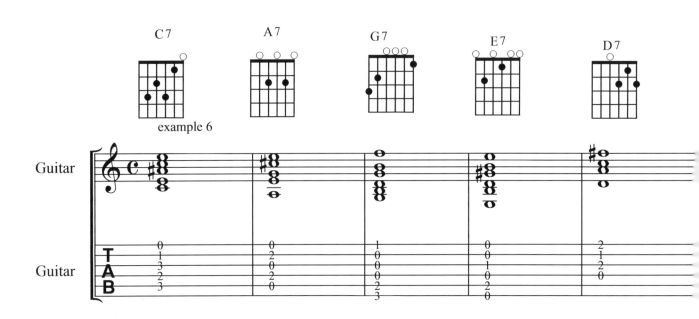

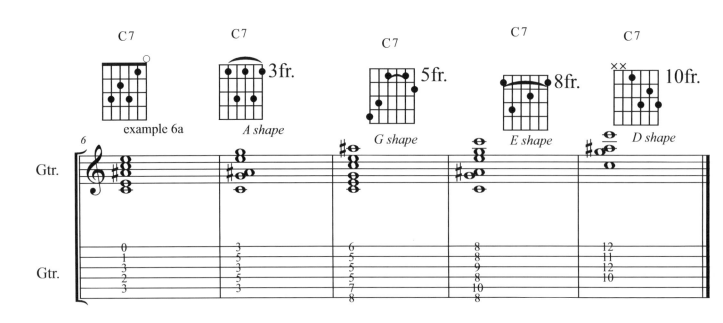

Key to the Highway

cd track 1

"Key to the Highway" is a classic eight bar blues in E written by Big Bill Broonzy. Let's take our CAGED knowledge and apply it to the E, A7 and B7 chords of this song. To start we can simply strum the three chords that you should already be familiar with. The chord changes come fairly quickly but you can play this song at a fairly moderate tempo –100bpm.

In the first variation we will replace the E chord with a D-shaped E7and the B7 and A7 with a G-shape. You may find these chord voicings less useful than the first position chords, especially if you are singing/playing these chords unaccompanied. But if you were playing with a band (bass, keys, drums) these new chord voicings can be used to create a new guitar part or solo.

The second variation uses shapes that have a fuller sound: E chord using a C-shape and the B7 and A7 chords using an E-shape. Note: throughout this book you will notice that the IV and V chords in a I IV V chord progression will use the same shape since they are usually close to each other.

The third variation moves the chord shapes up the neck: G-shape for the E chord and D-shape for the B7 and A7

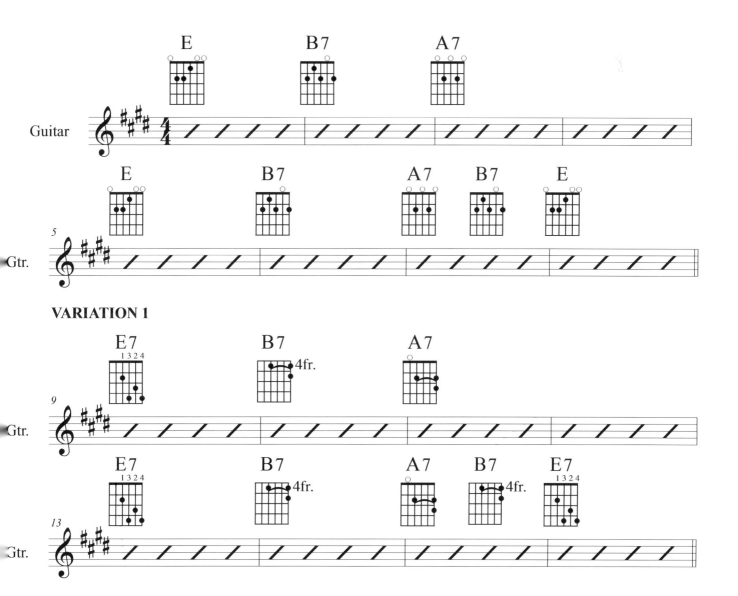

VARIATION 1

VARIATION 2

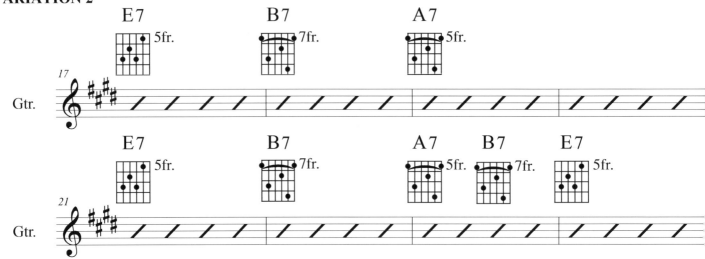

VARIATION 3

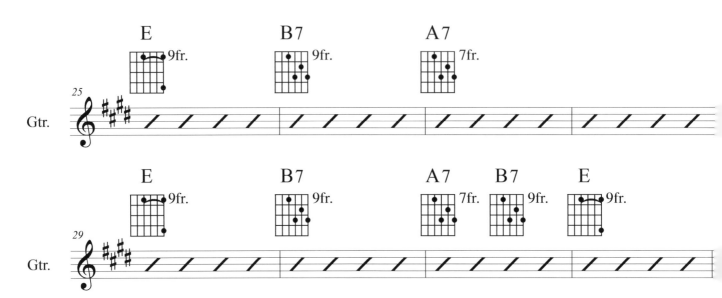

10

CHAPTER 2: SONGS

In this chapter we will:

• *learn Stagolee w/variations*

• *learn St. James Infirmary w/variations*

• *learn Train Stop Blues w/variations*

• *learn Cowboy Blues w/variations*

• *learn From Four Until Late w/variations*

• *learn Captain, Captain w/variations*

• *learn That'll Never Happen No More w/variations*

SECTION 2:
USING THE CAGED SYSTEM TO CREATE VERSE VARIATIONS

Okay, now we can start to have some fun with the CAGED system! Keep in mind that as you work your way through the songs presented here that a good way to approach each song will be to *strum* your way through each verse as you acquaint yourself with the new chord shapes. My students often want to jump right into the fingerpicking ,-- I appreciate their enthusiasm! – but this can make the process a little frustrating. By strumming the chords we are breaking the process down into sizable chunks: 1) left hand (fingering) familiarity, 2) fingerpicking. Most of the songs presented here are 12 bar blues. Break down each 12 bar section and learn the chords shapes with the strumming. Then work in the fingerpicking. You will find the process smoother if, as you work in the fingerpicking, you are already familiar with the chord shapes.

VARIATIONS

My system for creating the verse variations in these songs was to focus the chord shapes into a given 4-5fret range for any given verse: e.g. in the 2nd verse of Stag-o-lee the D/G/A chords are all fingered between the 5-7th frets. This makes our job easier and allows for a better flow between the chords. If we were to jump around the fretboard too much within a given verse the exercise becomes too much about finger calisthenics rather than keeping the flow of the music.

Whenever possible I will try to work open strings into the alternating bass patterns of my chord shapes – this is usually available to us with chords such as E A and D. This will lead us to come up with bass patterns that we may not have thought of before – for example, my original song "Stingy Brim," starts off with an interesting A chord that uses an open A string with a C# played on the 4th string/11th fret.

IMPROVISATION

Most of the improvisation in these verses is centered around what the various chord shapes offer us in the way of finger freedom. For instance, in the first variation of Stagolee the D chord is fingered in such a way as to allow the pinky freedom to grab notes on the first string. Again, whenever possible I will work open strings into the mix as this usually frees up a finger to navigate the possibilities within that shape. This may limit us to a certain extent. But this is also an opportunity to advance your chord knowledge as most of the embellishments we make to the melody/chord voicing involve adding 6ths, 9ths, 11ths, 13ths and chromatic runs.

Improvising for Fingerstyle Blues Guitar:
STAGOLEE
By
Pete Madsen
6/5/12

A while back I was teaching the Mississippi John Hurt song, "Stagolee" to one of my students and I realized that I could improvise over the chord changes by simply shifting the chord voicings up the fretboard. This brought new life to a song I had been playing for many years and gave me instrumental variations that could spice up the verses between vocal stanzas. My template for moving to the new voicings was the CAGED system: a system in which we take first position chord shapes (C – A –G – E- D) and move them up the neck to produce "new" chords.

For instance, if we take the first chord of "Stagolee", D, and apply CAGED shapes to it we can produce several new versions of the chord. In example 1 I have given you three versions of D. The first version should be familiar to anyone who has played the guitar before. The second uses an A-shaped chord – if you look at the fretboards you will notice I have shown two different shapes: the first shows you the entire shape and the second is an abbreviated shape that we will use in playing the song. The same goes for the third version of D, which uses a G-shaped chord but which I have shortened to make it more practical to play.

"Stagolee" is built around basic chord changes of a twelve bar blues in D with G and A as the IV and V chords. The G chord will sometimes be substituted with a G7, so we will look at both. Example 2a shows standard first position G and G7 chords. Example 2b shows a G7 chord with a D7 shape – notice that we will barre over the 5th and 4th strings in order to be able to use those strings in our alternating bass later on – and G chord using a C shape. Example 2c shows three versions of an A7: the first will be used in the first verse of "Stagolee" and the other two will be used in the subsequent verses. The third A7 chord in this example is the same as the G7 in example 2b but leaves the 5th string open so that we can use the A note in our bass pattern.

Critical to Hurt's playing style is his consistent alternating bass patterns, so I have used chord variations that will sustain this kind of groove. For instance, in example 3a we have a basic fingerpicking pattern that we would use over the first position D chord (*notice that we use the open A string as our first and third bass note in each measure, which is the 5th of D and not the root). In example 3b I am able to keep the same bass pattern over a higher voiced A-shaped D chord. In example 3c the bass pattern is altered slightly (second and fourth beats get an octave A note) over the shortened G-shaped D chord.

Keep in mind that when I play a verse of "Stagolee" I will not be moving between these various D chords. On the contrary, during each verse I will strive to keep my chord shapes within a limited range of frets so that I don't have to move around too much and can keep the flow of the song. In example 4 you can see that the move from D to G keeps us in the same range between the 5th-7th frets.

Likewise, for our transition from D to A; by using an abbreviated version of an E-shaped A7 chord (traditional barre chord) I am able to keep the same 5-7th fret range as shown in example 5.

Before we go on to play "Stagolee" I would like to point out that what you do with these chord shapes leaves a lot of room for interpretation and, thus, improvisation. You can embellish the chords by adding hammer-ons, pull-offs and open strings. It doesn't take too much imagination to come up with some neat runs. For instance, I can take the D chord from example 3b and "play" around with it to produce variations. In example 6 we take a four measure section and play different notes on the first string. In the first measure we start by playing the E string open which produces a D9 chord. In the second measure we play a pull-off from the 5th fret to the open string. Then, in the third measure we play a descending melody line which produces D7 – D6 – D chords. Finally, we finish off by repeating the second measure in this sequence. As you go through the verses of "Stagolee" that I have laid out try to think of other ways you can embellish the chords.

STAGOLEE

We will play three different verses for "Stag-O-Lee." The first is the standard verse Hurt would play and sing over. The second will be our first CAGED-derived variation, which I think fits well as an instrumental break. The next verse can also function as an instrumental break. After playing the first verse ala John Hurt I moved up to the 5th position A-shaped D chord – a common barre chord shape. But instead of barring I kept the 5th and 4th strings open and simply played the top three strings (1-3) fretted, which allowed me to use my little finger to perform a nice pull-off on the 1st string from the 7th-5th frets – see 1st 4 bars of *first variation*. When I got to the G7 chord I was able to stay in the same space (5-7th fret) and use a D-shaped G7 (measures 5-7). Back to the D, then to A7 in the same 5-7 fret range; this time the A7 is a shortened version of an E-shaped A7, where we only barre the top four strings and play the 5th string open.

Our second variation will use a G-shaped D chord -- which I will shorten so that I can finger it easier and still use the 5th string open A in my bass pattern, -- a C-shaped G chord; and a D-shaped A7 chord. One of the things I like about this variation is you do not have to move your left hand index finger. You can actually keep the index finger on the 7th fret, barring the top four strings for the D chord. You can still keep the barre in place for the G chord (this time we use a G instead of a G7). You can even keep the barre over the A chord, although its only fretting one string (the 4th) and is not necessary for sounding any other strings.

Improvising for Fingerstyle Blues Guitar

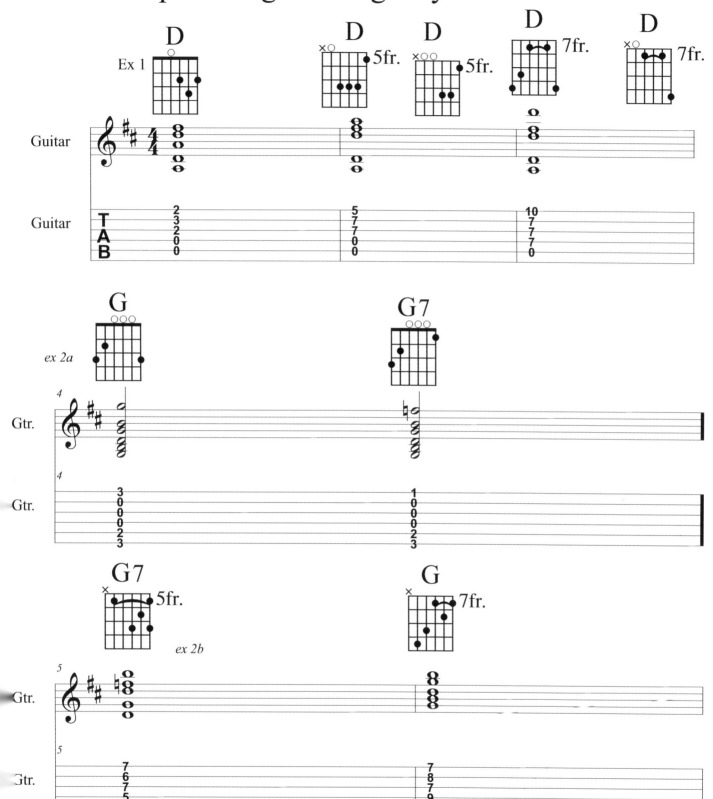

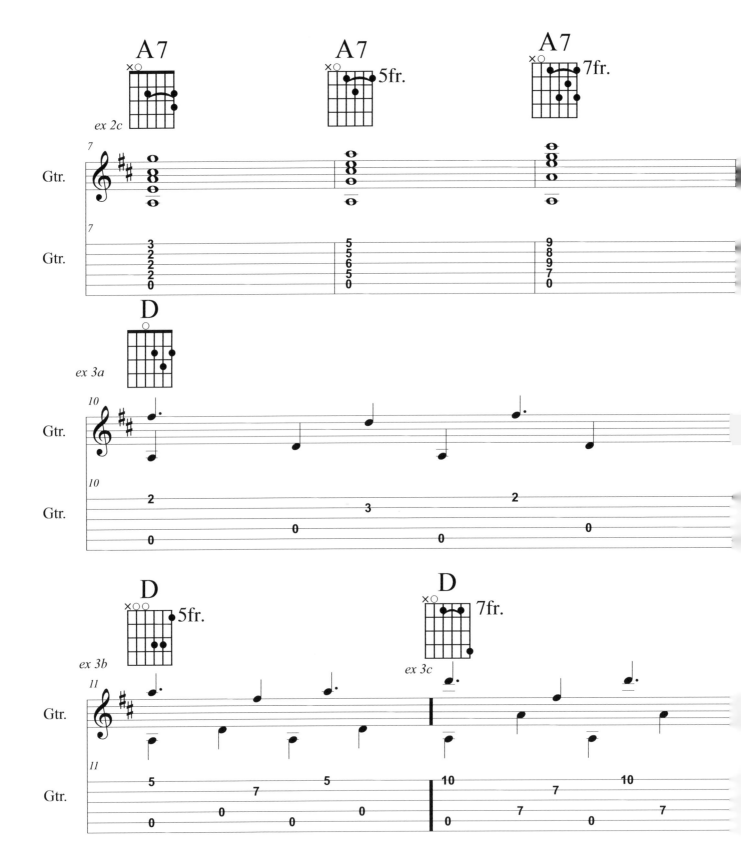

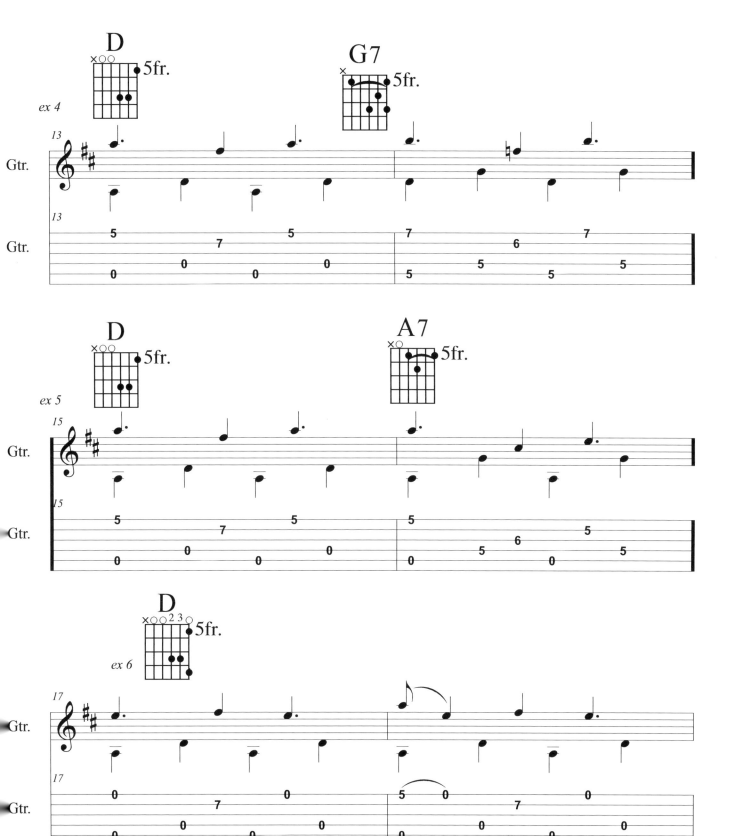

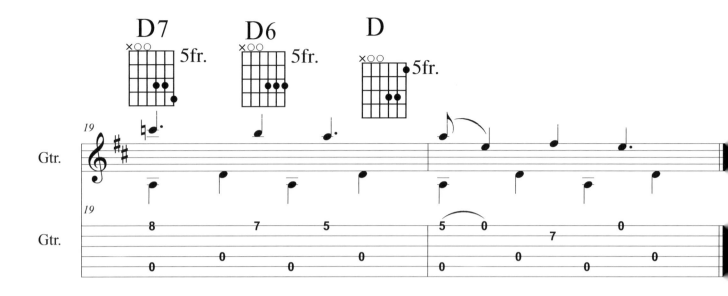

Strumming Chord Changes

For each song I present in this book you will see a simple chart of the chord changes. It's always a good idea to familiarize your self with the changes and where they occur. You should strum through these changes before going on to working on the fingerpicking examples.

Think of this as a warm-up for your left hand. When you have practiced this a few times you will know when to expect the changes and will be able to get your left hand in position. Then you can focus on the finger picking. I haven't mapped out all the chord changes for the variations presented, but you can do the same thing: strum through the variations and get your left hand fingerings down before moving on to finger picking.

Stagolee Chord Changes

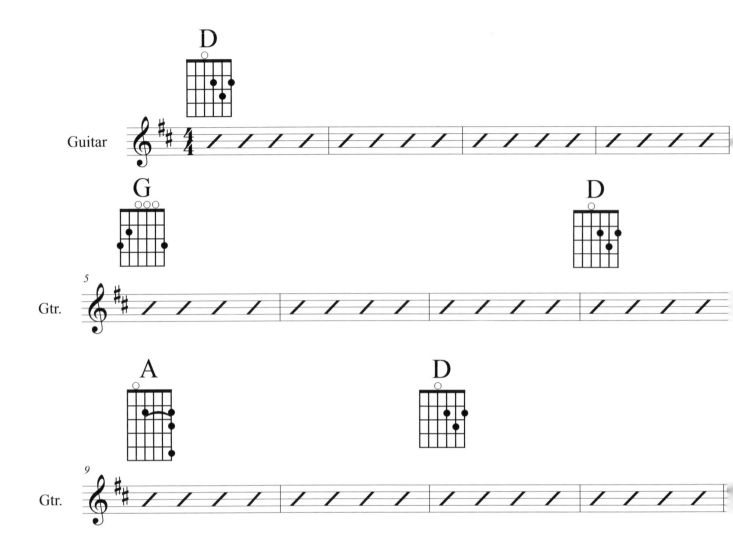

Stagolee

cd track 3

Example 2 - Stagolee

One day, as I was playing the John Hurt song, "Stagolee" with one of my students, I stumbled on some nifty variations for the chords D-G-A using CAGED ideas. After playing the first verse ala John Hurt I moved up to the 5th position A-shaped D chord - a common barre chord shape. But instead of barring I kept the 5th and 4th strings open and simply played the top three strings (1-3) fretted, which allowed me to use my little finger to perform a nice pull-off on the 1st string from the 7th-5th frets - see 1st 4 bars of first variation. When I got to the G7 chord I was able to stay in the same space (5-7th fret) and use a D-shaped G7 (measures 5-7). Back to the D, then to A7 in the same 5-7 fret range; this time the A7 is a shortened version of an E-shaped A7, where we only barre the top four strings and play the 5th string open.

A second variation could use a G-shaped D chord, which I would shorten so that I could finger it easier and still use the 5th string open A in my bass pattern; a C-shaped G chord (this could also be a G7 like the Cowboy Blues example); and a D-shaped A7 chord

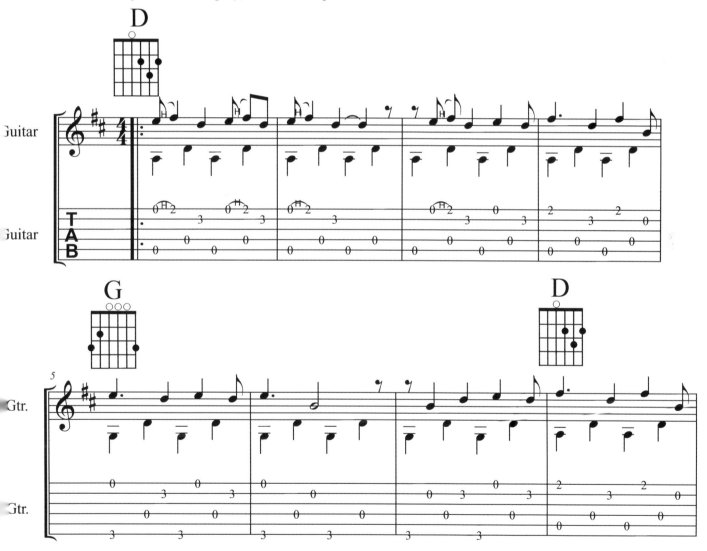

21

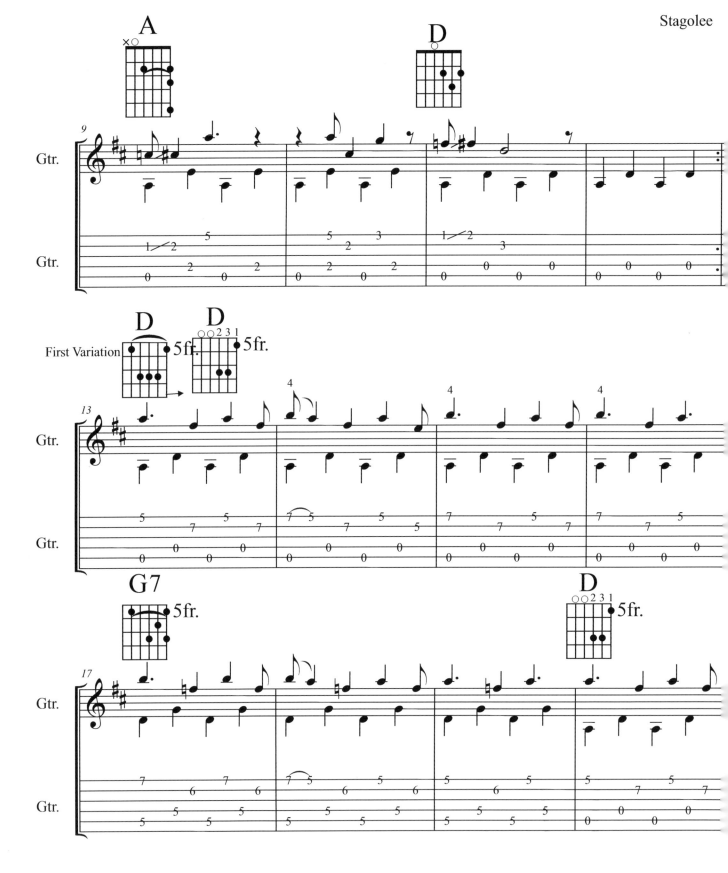

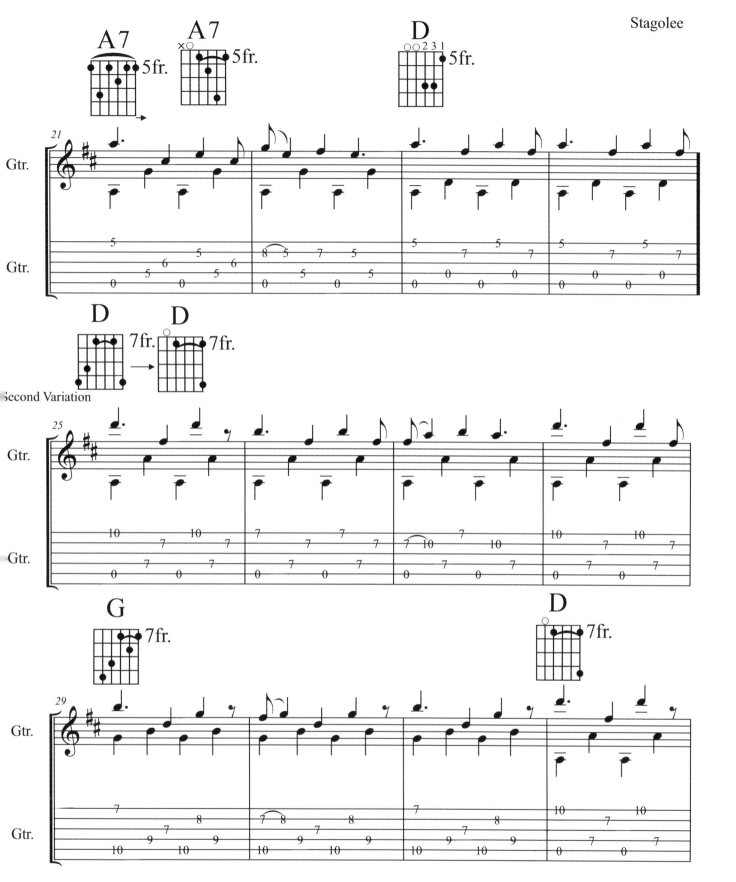

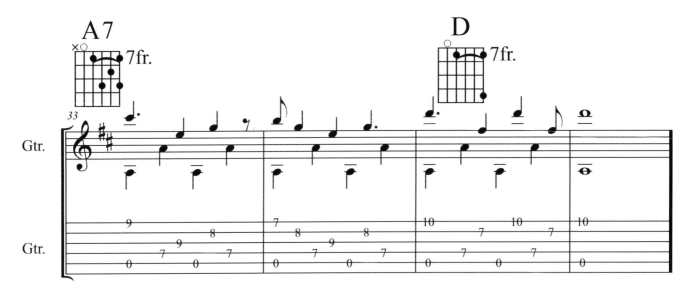

FURTHER IDEAS FOR IMPROV:

Pull-offs and hammer-ons are our friends! In the first bar of this run we pull-off from the first string 5th fret to the open E string, yielding a D9 chord. Pulling-off from the 8th fret adds the flat 7th in; and then the 8th fret from the 2nd string adds in a suspended 4th.

CHROMATICISM:

In this example we take the G7 chord voicing from the second verse and play a descending run on the first and then the second string, followed by a hammer-on lick in the third bar

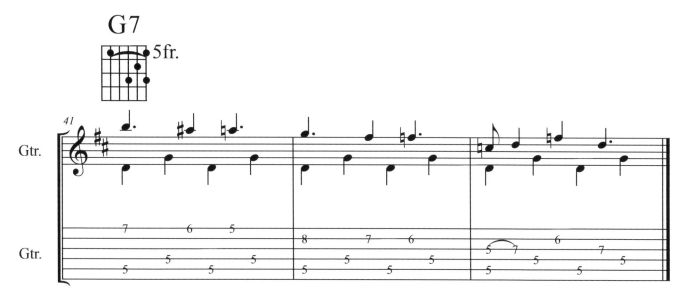

St. James Infirmary

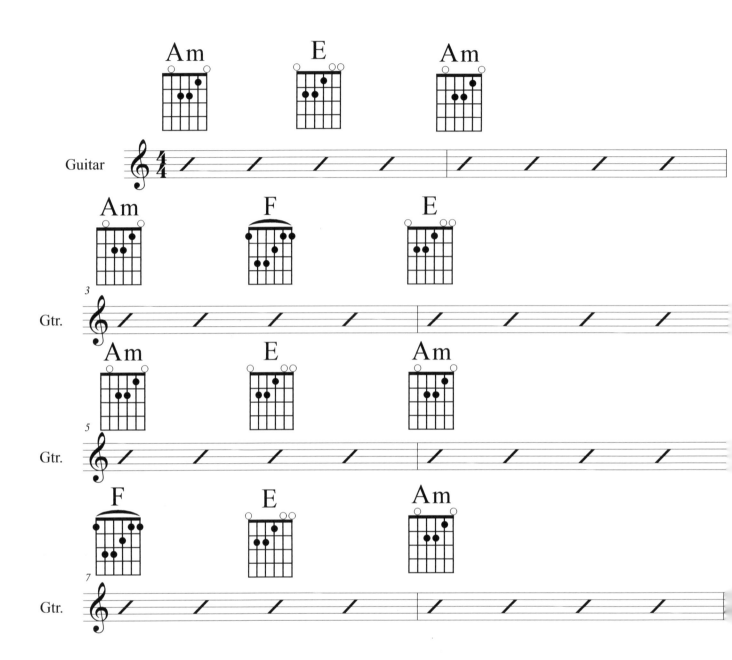

St. James Infirmary

St. James Infirmary has two new components: 1) It is an eight bar blues (as opposed to the 12 bar form we have been dealing with); 2) and it uses a minor chord (Am). I find the A, E and D shapes of minor chords much more useful than the C and G shapes. For that reason we will only deal with the AED shapes in the three verses of St. James presented here. We will use the same alternating bass as before. The first verse is self-explanatory. The second verse shifts the A minor to an E-shape, then quickly to the C-shape E. One tip, as you move between these chords, is to keep your index finger on your fretting hand barring the top three strings and then moving down one fret to get to the E major chord. The third verse emlpoys a D-shape A minor and a G-shaped E and F chords.

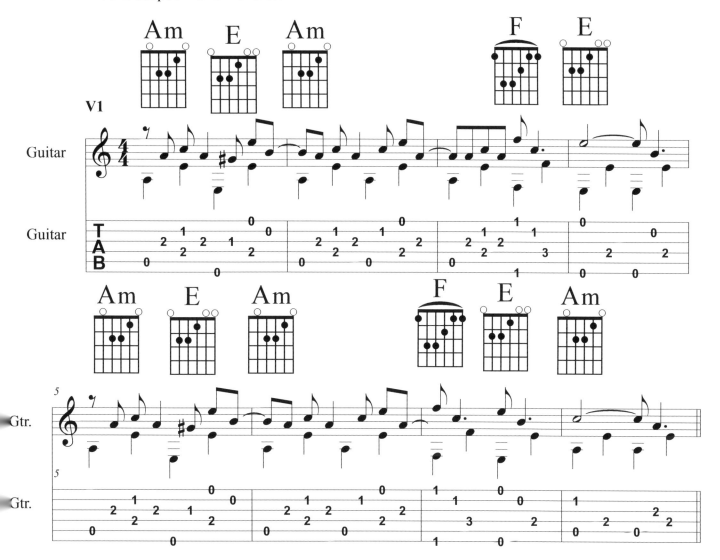

St. James Infirmary

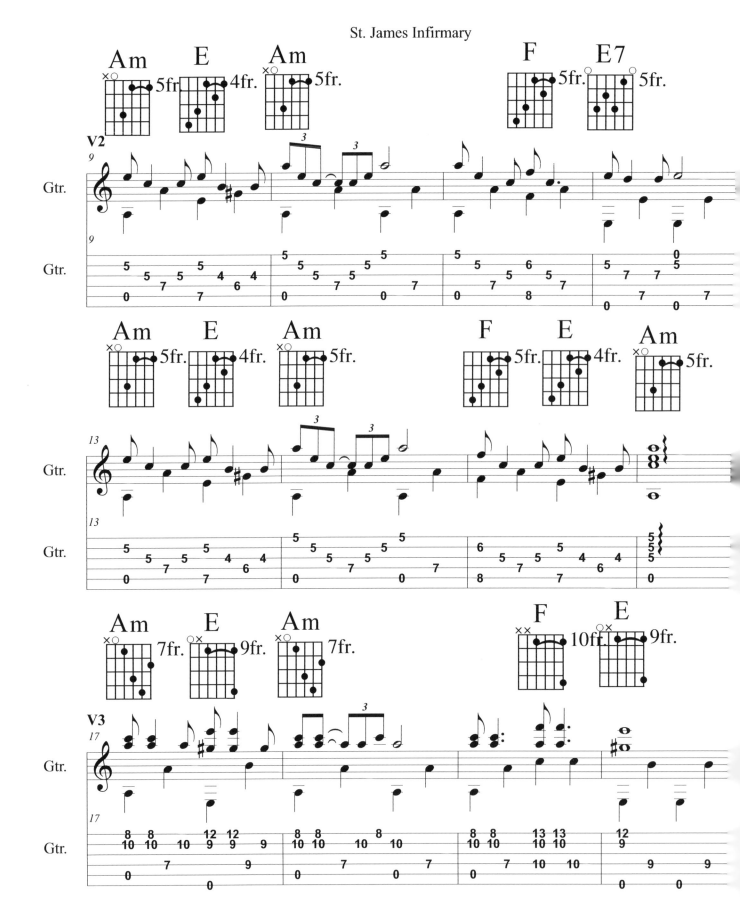

28

St. James Infirmary

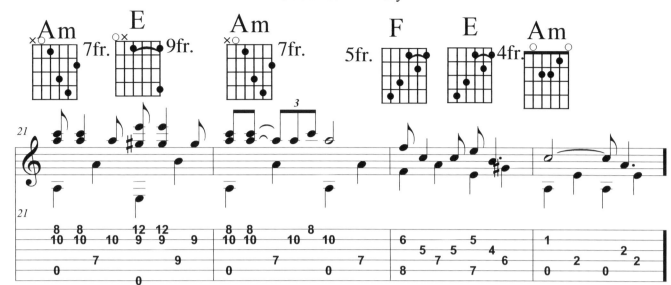

FURTHER IDEAS FOR IMPROV:
The chord changes in St. James come fairly quickly, so the best place for a little improv is over measures 3-4, where we spend a little more time on the A minor. Using the E shape A minor from m the 2nd verse we walk up the second string to form an A minor 6, then an A minor 7th.

CHROMATICISM:
or we can walk up the same string but add in the #5 at the 6th fret

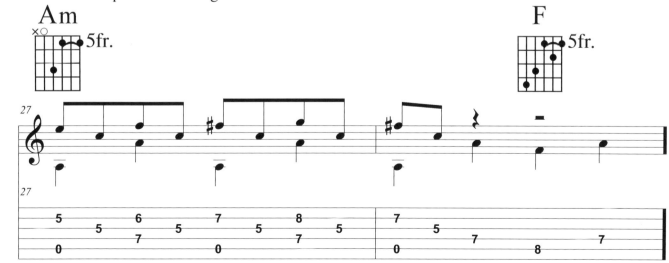

MORE PULL-OFFS:
Here again the pinky will grab notes up the neck to produce pull-offs -- when the pinky leaves the second string from the d-shaped A minor chord the 7th fret on the 2nd string produces an A minor 6 chord

Train Stop Blues -- Chord Changes

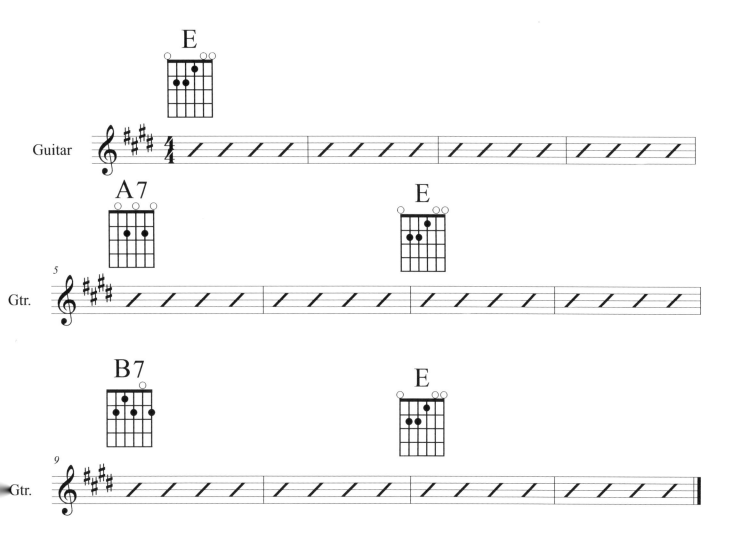

Train Stop Blues:
w/improv

cd track 5

Some of you may remember "Train Stop Blues" from one of my earlier lessons. I use it to teach the alternating bass over blues chord changes. We will start out with the original first verse from that lesson; then create two NEW verses using CAGED ideas. In the second verse we start off with a C-shaped E chord: notice that I show you two versions of the chord: the first one shows you the "parent" chord; and the second is the "altered" chord I use to play the verse. The parent chord is an obvious C-shape, but I alter it by leaving off the 5th string and adding my pinky to the first string. This allows me to come up with some nice melodic ideas that I use throughout the verse. The parent chord for the A7 is a typical E-shaped barre chord, but I like to shorten it so that I am only barring four strings, while leaving the 5th (A) string open. The B chord is based on a G-shape, but this time I shorten it simply because the full version is too hard to play!

   The third verse moves farther up the neck starting with a G-shaped E chord; then a C-shaped A7, and a D-shaped B7 chord

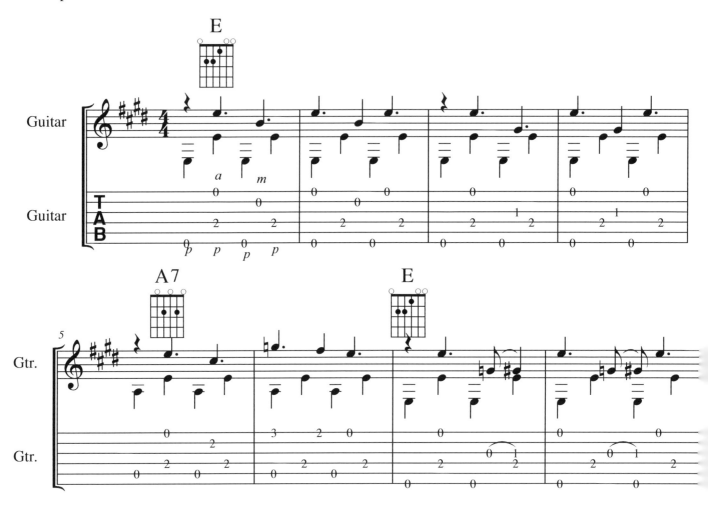

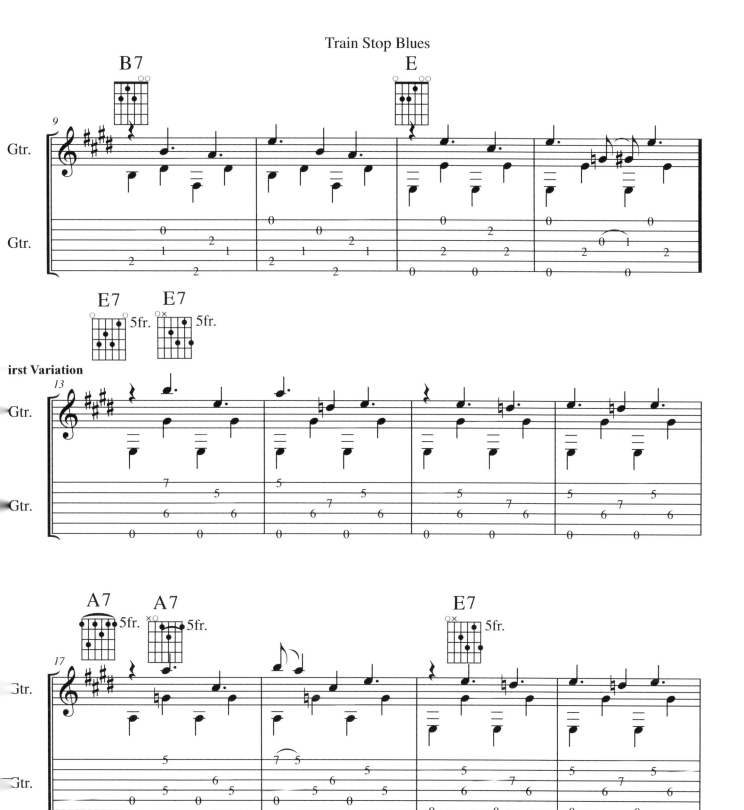

Train Stop Blues

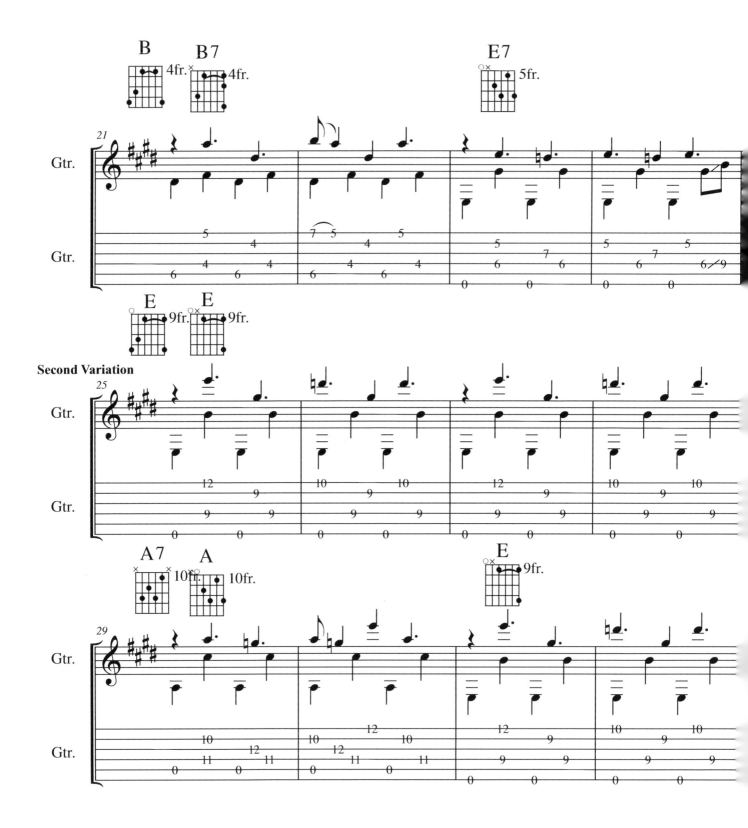

34

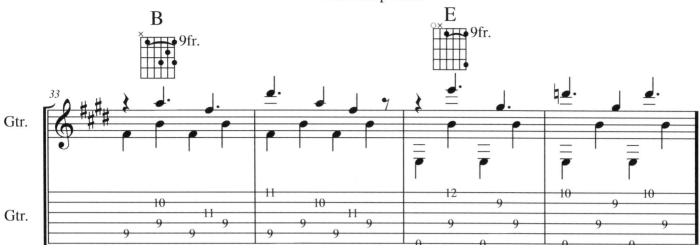

MORE IDEAS FOR IMPROV:

Pull-offs and chromaticism are demonstrated over our 2nd verse C-shaped E chord in the example below. After the pull-off in the 2nd measure we ascend from the G# (major 3rd of E) one fret at a time up to B (the perfect 5th of E)

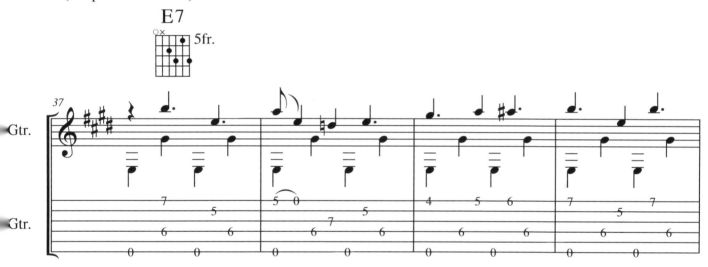

MORE CHROMATICISM;

Of course, we are not limted to ascending or descending chromatically on just one string. In the example below we use the G-shaped E chord to descend on the first string and then the second string, before ascending back up the second string.

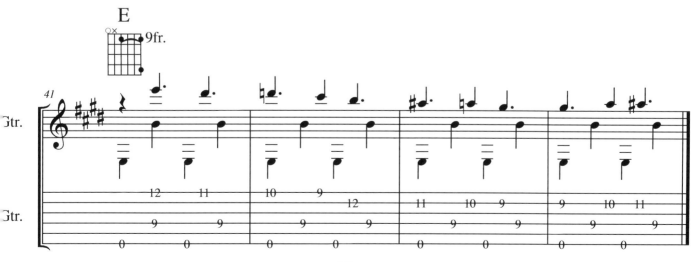

Cowboy Blues -- Chord Changes

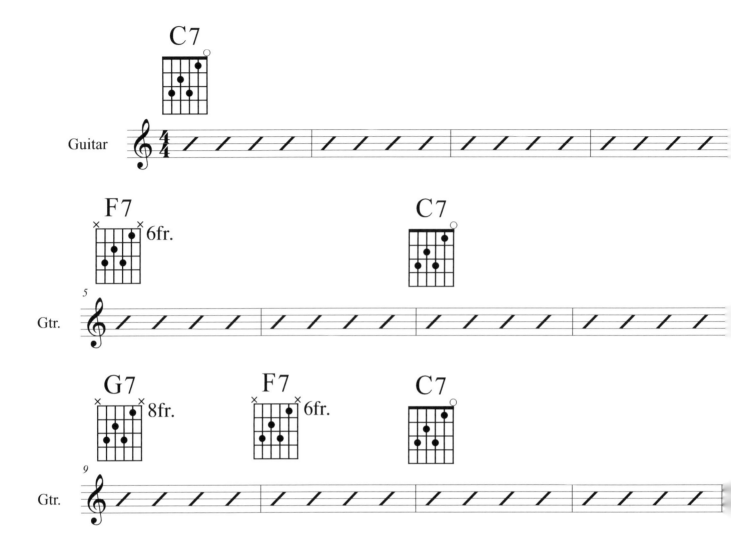

Cowboy Blues Improv

The following 12 bar blues starts off by exploiting the C-shaped C7 chord. Another apsect to the CAGED system is that we can use the SAME chord shape to play all the chords in a I-IV-V sequence. In this case the F7 and G7 chords use the same chord shape (moved up the neck) as the C7 chord. This makes it easier to maintain the bass pattern (5/4/6/4) for all the chords. In the second verse we go for a more straight forward bass pattern (5/4/5/4) that allows us to play around with the chord shapes. The C7 uses an A-shape, then the F7 uses a D-shape. Notice that when we move back to the C7 chord we use diffrent shapes to create a descending run that resolves back to the first position C7.
In the third verse we move up the neck, using chord shapes typical of what Merle Travis would play.

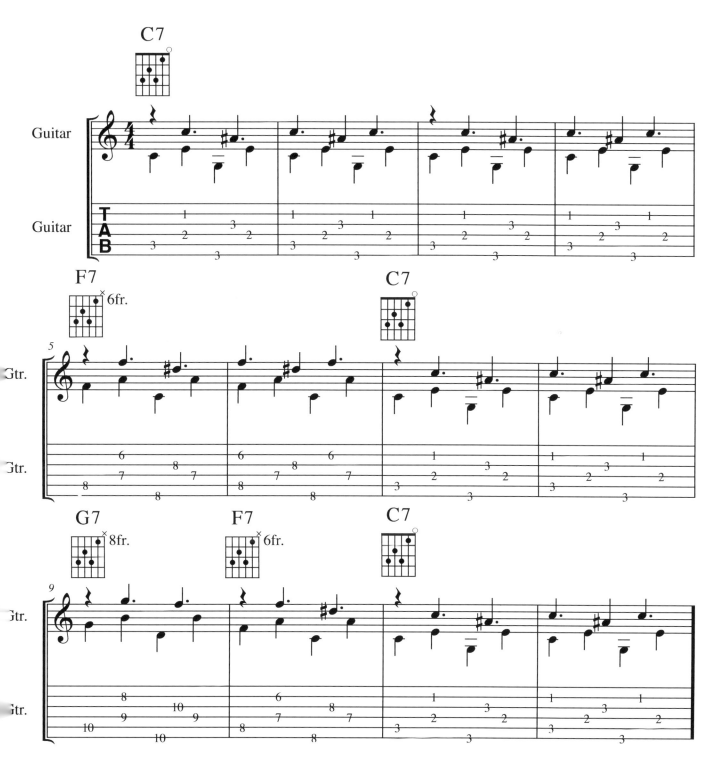

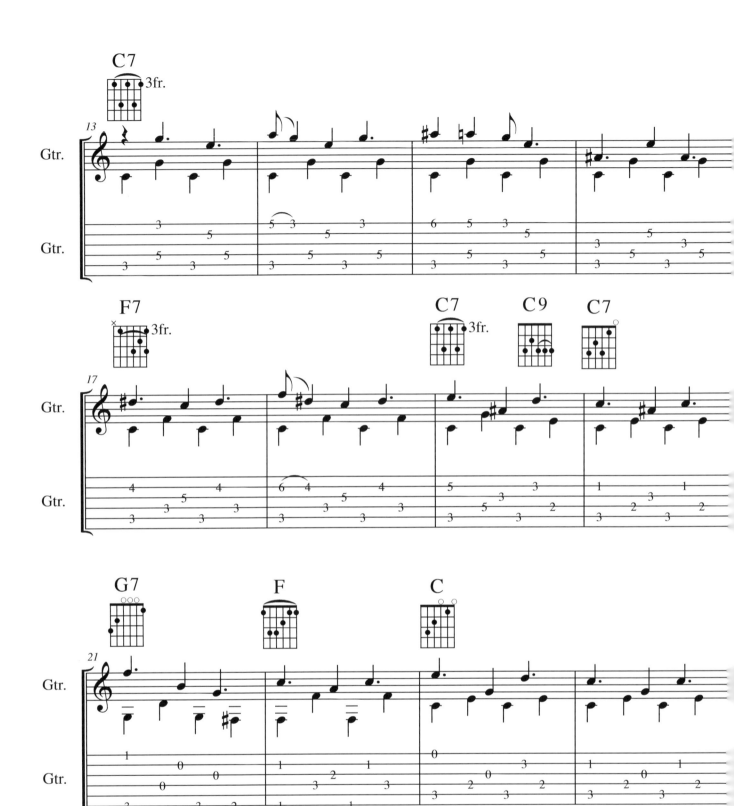

MORE IDEAS FOR IMPROVISATION:

Borrowing ideas from other songs -- in this case, "Freight Train" -- is another way to improvise. Moving the pinky around is a great way to go, but the first move in the example below involves dropping the middle finger from the 4th string down to the third string, creating a C6 chord and disrupting the bass pattern slightly with a D note played on the 4th string instead of E. Sounds good. The next 3 measures are just a matter of moving the pinky around.

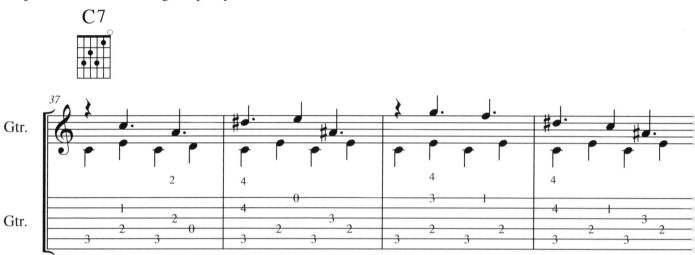

CHROMATICISM AND BASS FUN:

Using your thumb to fret bass notes -- like in the example below and form the third verse of "Cowboy Blues"-- frees up more fingers to improvise with. In the chromatic descending run in the measure 41 and 43 below you will be using your pinky, then your third finger to fret the notes at the 10th and 9th frets. In measure 44 you can use your index finger to pluck the 4th string pull-off.

40

From Four Until Late -- Chord Changes

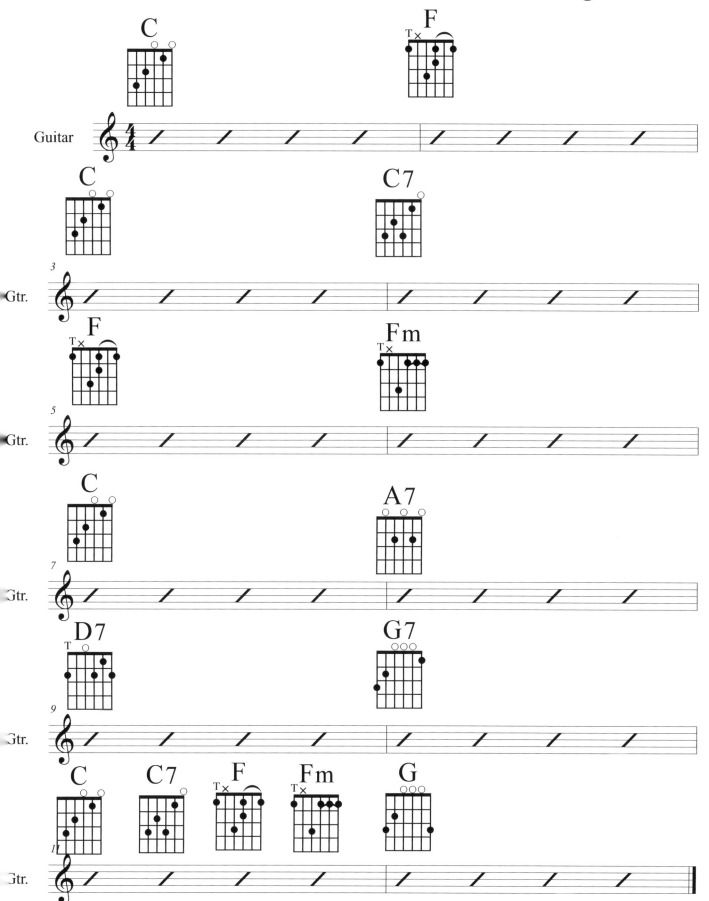

From Four Until Late

Robert Johnson

This 12 bar blues by Robert Johnson has some really nice touches. First, we have the quick change from C to
F, measure 1-2. This is one of those songs where you will want to use your left hand thumb to fret the 6th
string bass note for the F chord. In the third measure we have a riff based on chromatic descending parallel
thirds. We see this twice: the first time it resolves back to a C chord. The second time, in measure 8, it resolv
to an A7. Also, the IV chord in measures 4-5 moves from a major (F) to a F minor - a move that is used agai
in the turnaround, measure 11, where we move from C-C7-F-F minor. This is a harmonically more fleshed o
version of the RJ turnaround used in songs like "Kind Hearted Woman," and "Crossroads." I gave this song
more regular bass pattern than Johnson would normally play.

The one variation uses an E-shaped C chord with your thumb over the fretboard, then a quick change
to a C-shaped F chord, before returning to the same C chord. The F-Fm change use A-shaped chords. In the
turnaround we use "smaller" chords, fretted on the top three strings to produce the quick series of changes.

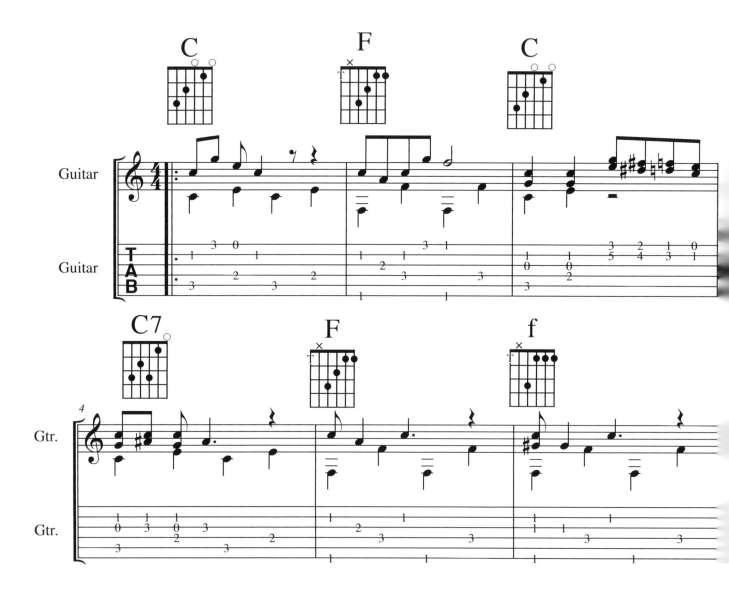

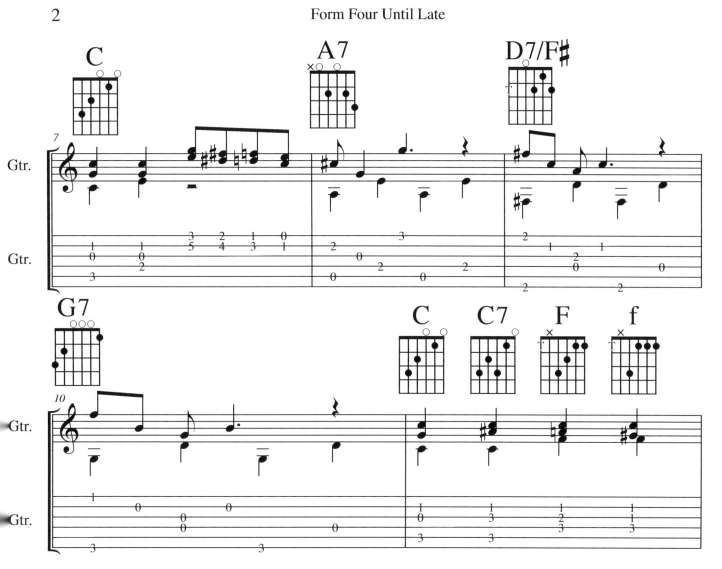

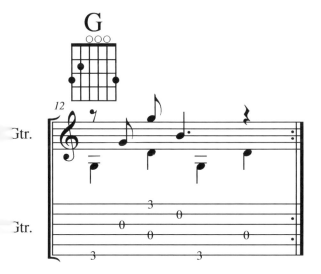

4

Form Four Until Late

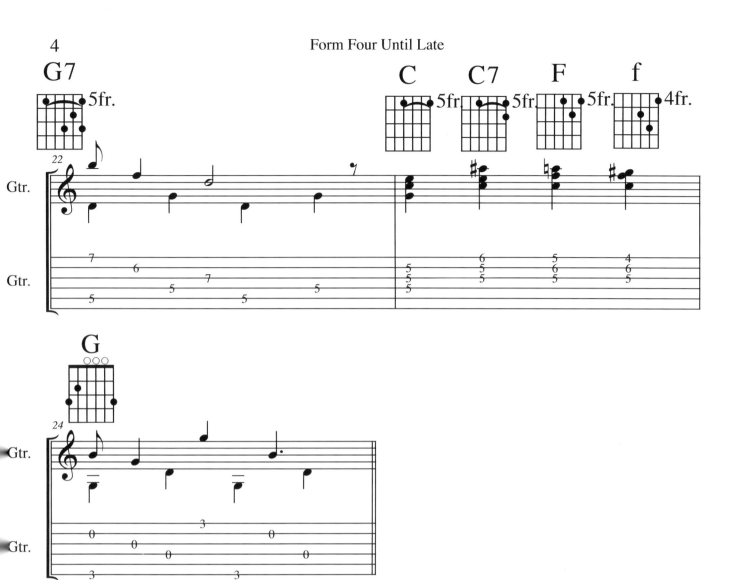

45

Captain, Captain -- Chord Changes

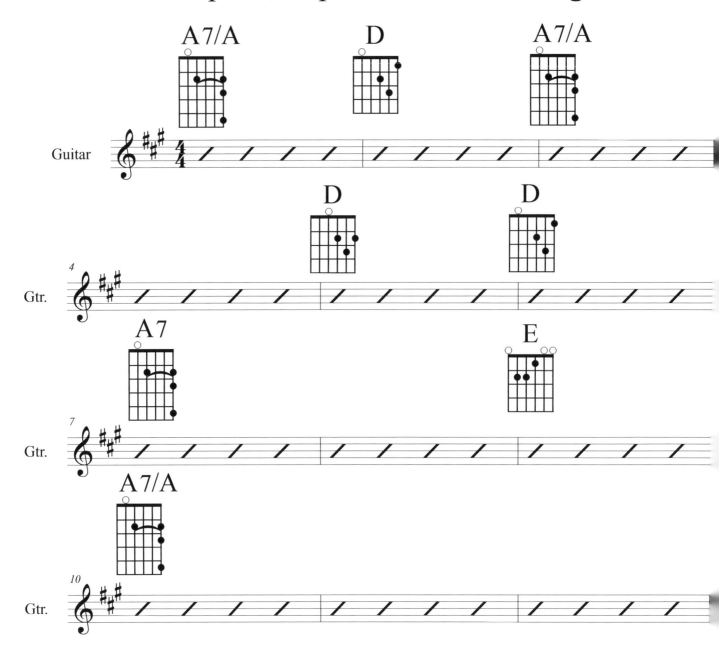

Captain, Captain
w/variations

Mance Lipscomb

This Mance Lipscomb song uses a monotonic bass pattern in the key of A. The first thing you will notice as you play through the opening verse is that Mance will stay on the A string even when he shifts to a D chord. In fact, the only time he leaves the A bass is when he moves to the V (E) chord. The A and A7 chords in this verse are G-shaped-based. The D chord is a strange mix of major and minor tonalities – although I think the F note is more of a tickle than a settled note. The central lick in this song occurs in the 3rd measure and returns in the 10th and 11th bar.

The opening phrase in the 1st variation captures the same opening lick in an E-shaped position instead of the G-shape from the prior verse. The first D chord in this verse uses an A-shape. Returning to the A in measure 15 requires a quick pinky move from the 8th fret on the 2nd string to the 8th fret on the 3rd string. The next D chord becomes a D7 using a G-shape. Back at A in measure 19 we use a slight variation on a D-shape. The E7 chord is a thinly disguised D-shape – I have placed a G# (major third of E) in the bass to mix things up a bit. It makes sense to come back to the original A chord lick from the first verse so that is how we wrap up this second verse.

In the third verse we move up the neck and toggle between a C-shaped A chord and an E-shaped D chord. The E-shape once again requires us to use the thumb over the neck to fret the 6th string. We can then add the hammer-on lick that will become a central part of this verse. The E chord in this verse bridges two shapes – the G# and the D on the 4th and 3rd strings are part of a C-shape and the E note played on the 3rd string/9th fret is part of an A-shape.

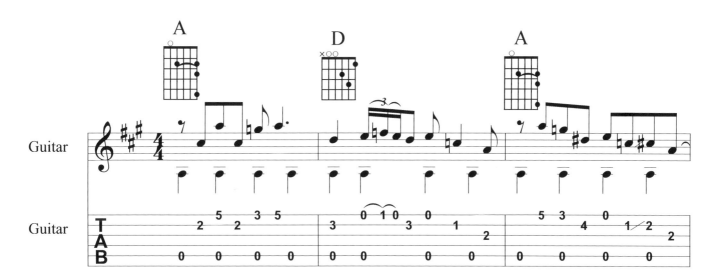

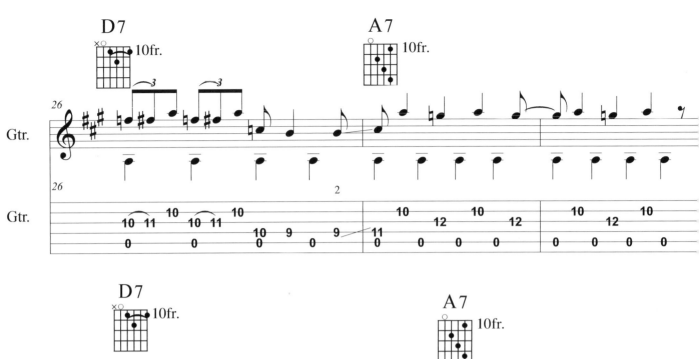

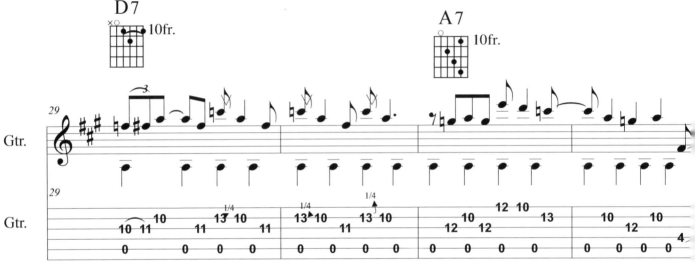

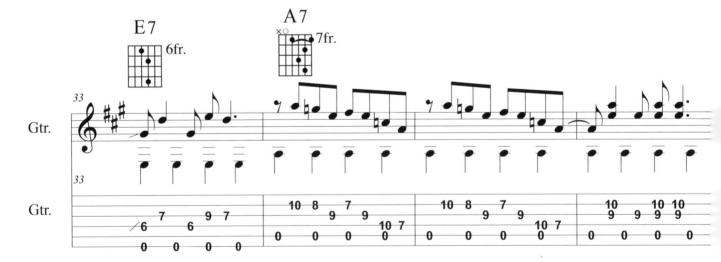

That'll Never Happen No More -- Chord Changes

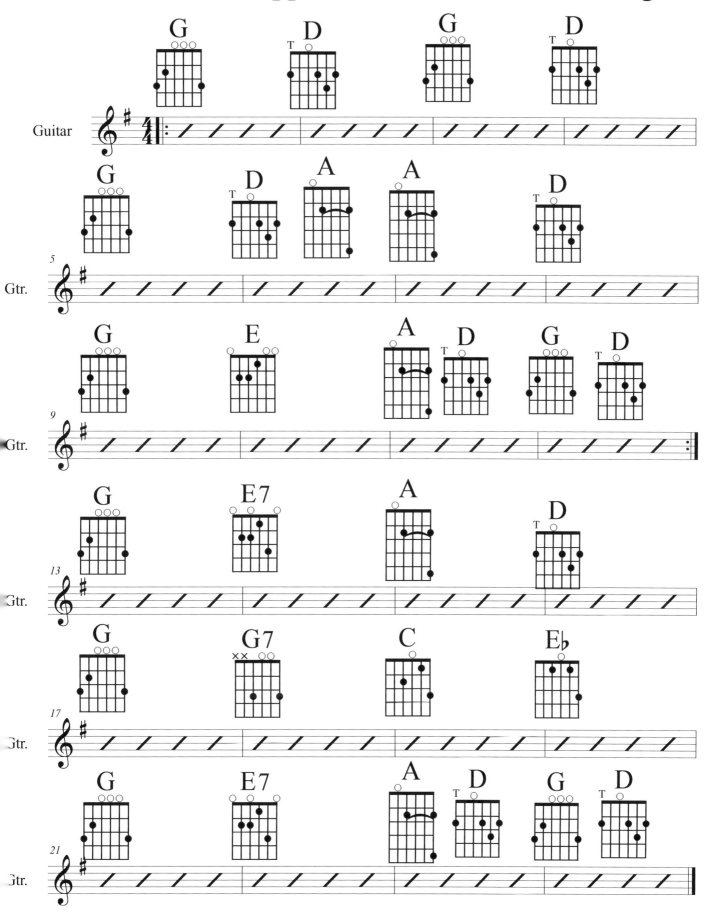

That'll Never Happen No More

Blind Blak

arrange
Pete Madse

This Blind Blake song has a distinctly ragtime feel. It moves quickly between the chords so take your time before bringing it up to speed. The first six bars moves back and forth between G and D. In bar 6 we creep up to a G-shaped A chord – use your pinky to navigate between the 3rd and 5th frets. Typical of Blind Blake songs are what I like to call "bass hiccups." At the end of bar 13 Blake moves to an E7 chord and he anticipates the chord by playing a 6th string bass note on the and of 4 and then landing on the 5th string. In bars 17-20 there is a roll and stop feel (make sure to listen to the recording).

Starting in measure 25 we go with our CAGED alternative verse variation. I got to admit I had some fun coming up with this one! The first E-shaped G chord should be played with your thumb fretting the 6th string; this allows your first finger to toggle between the 1st and 2nd strings and to play the pull-offs. Quickly move to the C-shaped D chord, then use your pinky and 1st finger to play the double pull-off. In measure 28 the implied chord is D, but I use just the 5th and 4th string bass notes of a C-shape chord to move from C up to D. Measures 31-32 has us playing an E-shaped A chord and then playing a partial A-shape D chord which descends to a partial D9. In measure 34 we play a C-shape E7 chord that walks the melody down from the 7th fret/1st string to the 5th, 4th fret then open.

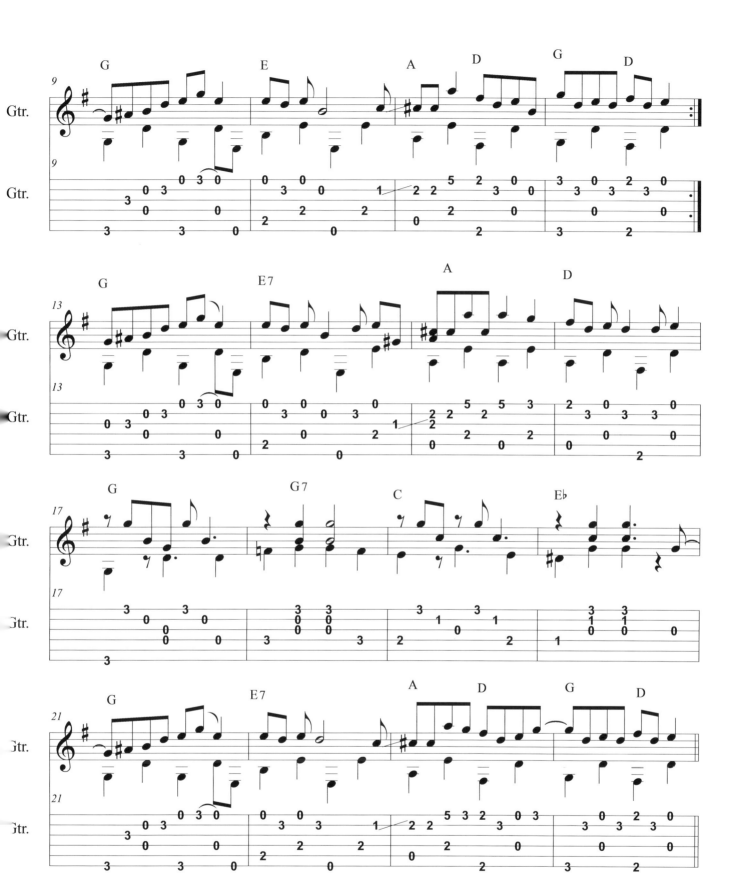

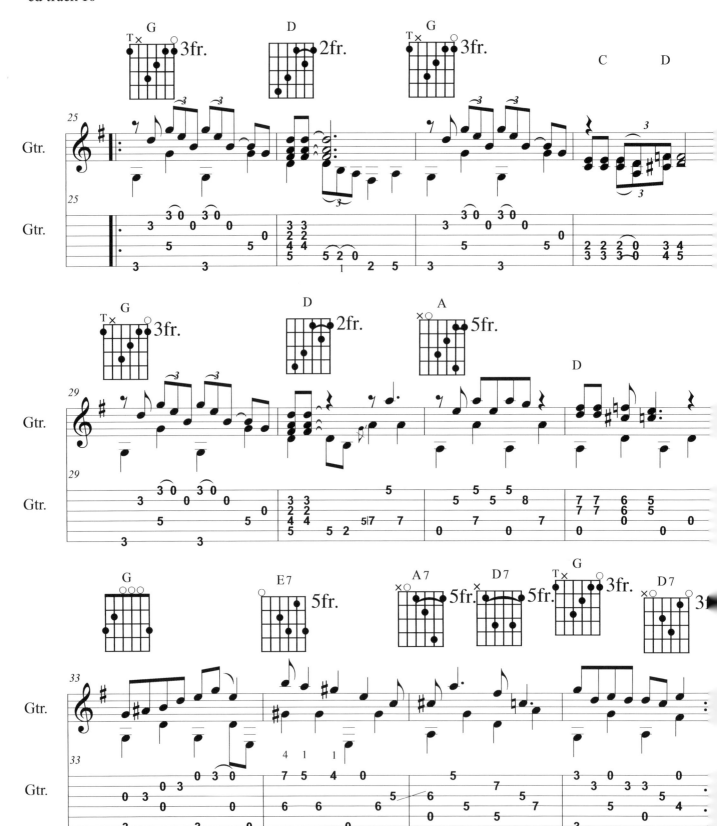

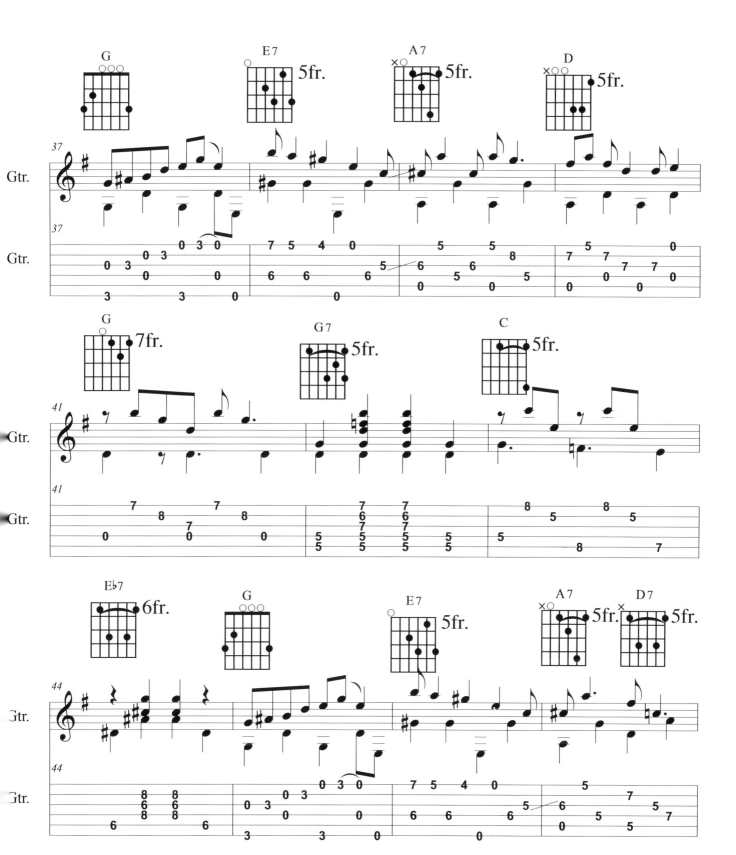

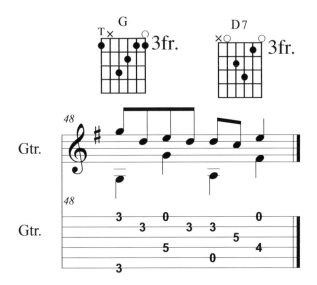

CHAPTER 3:
Dropped D Tuning

In this chapter we will:

• *use dropped D tuning and apply CAGED system examples to three songs*

   • *Big Road Blues*

   • *Badlands*

   • *Stingy Brim*

Introduction to Dropped D Tuning

Dropped D Tuning (DADGBE) gives us an opportunity to add a low resonant D note to our sound pallet, while retaining most of the CAGED shapes from standard tuning (from the 5th string down, anyways). For those of you unfamiliar with this tuning all you have to do is tune the 6th string down one whole step from E to D. You now have a lower register note that can be combined with your other D string (the 4th string) to form an alternating bass pattern or a drone. The slackened string also has a more haunting sound

Remember, all your CAGED patterns will be available from the 5th string down. The songs Big Road Blues and Stingy Brim use a lot of CAGED ideas. However, Badlands, which is an original tune, has less of a CAGED aura hanging over it.

Big Road Blues

dropped D tuning: DADGBE

Tommy Johnson

Pete Madsen

Big Road Blues, penned by Tommy Johnson in the late 1920s has a funky edge. The opening bass-driven riff is similar to what Bootsy Collins and Larry Graham would play decades later as bass players in funk driven bands like Parliament Funkaldelic and Sly and the Family Stone. In part, dropped D tuning lends itself to this kind of phrasing because the 4th and 6th strings line up in parallel. The G7 chord voicing used in bar 5-6 and returned to throughout is very common for this tuning. Upon returning to the I chord (D) in measures 7-8 there is a cool sounding shift between the D chord and a diminished chord, which is repeated in measures 11-12.

In our first variation we will use an abbreviated G-shaped D chord with a descending melody line mostly played by the pinky, which produces a slightly discordant juxtaposition between the minor and major third (3rd string/10th fret against 2nd string/7th fret). When we get to the IV chord (G7), in the 17th measure, you will notice that we are using an E-shape, but since we are in open D tuning the bass note is played two frets above where it normally is. In the last four bars of this variation we will use a walking bass line (ascending over A/ descending over G), and then return to the D/D diminished lick.

The third variation starts off with a lick based around our normal D chord voicing. In order to translate this lick over to the G chord we have to do a bit of finger stretching. Back at the D chord in measure 31 we turn the tables by making the bass become the active section and the treble being static.

Big Road Blues

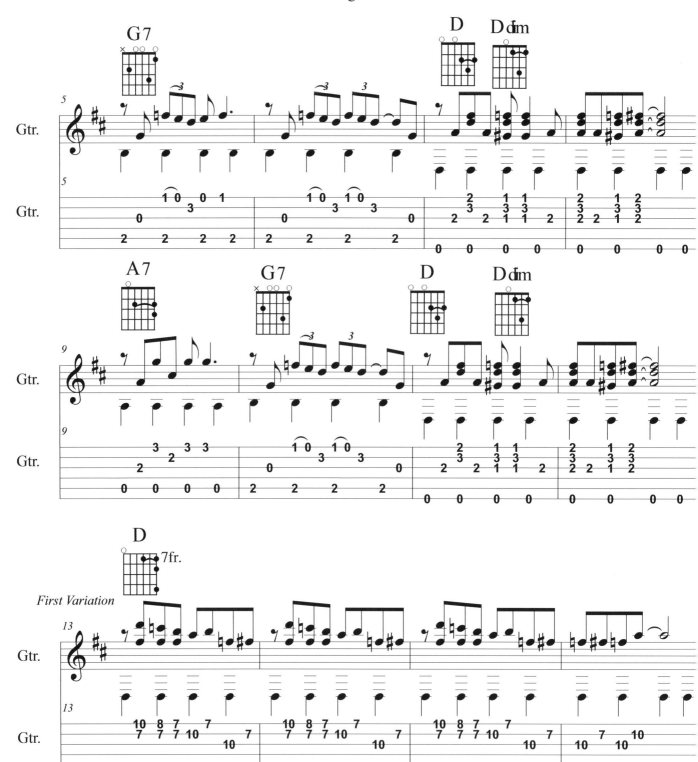

60

Big Road Blues

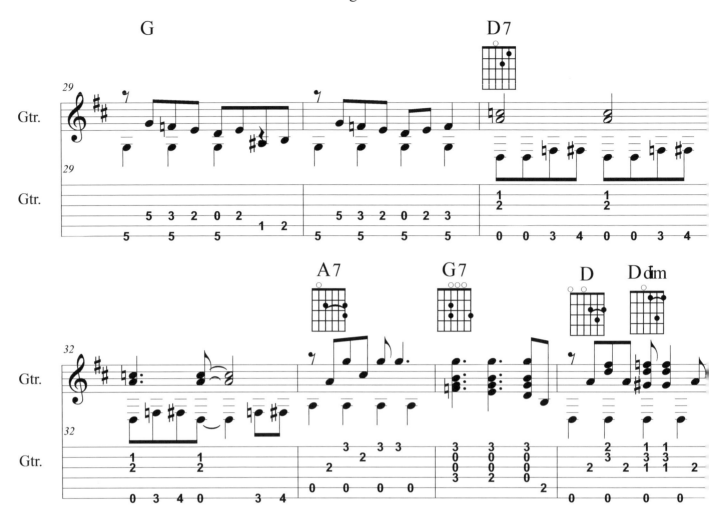

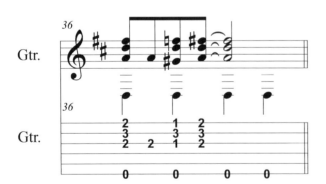

62

IDEAS FOR IMPORIVISATION: dominant 7th scale
The first 4 bars of Big Road Blues are ripe for improvisation. In this example we will use a different tactic: a dominant 7th scale

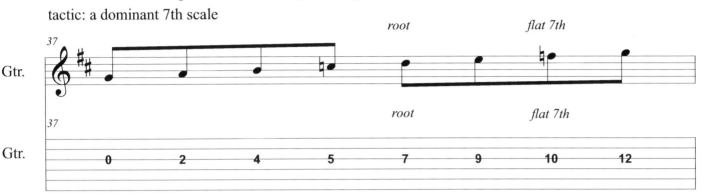

Now we can use both the 6th and 4th strings, which are tuned to D, for a fat droning sound...and adding scale tones produces this cool run that will lead us nicely into the G7 chord in the 5th bar of the 12 bar pattern. Play around with these scale tones and produce your own cool-sounding run!

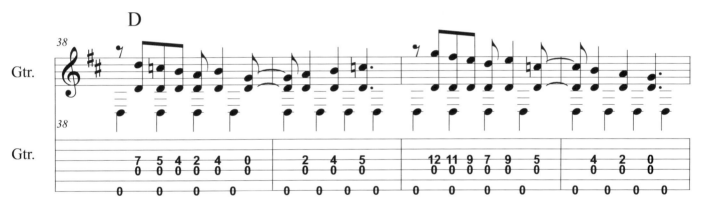

MAJOR PENTATONIC SCALE:
The major pentatonic scale can also be an ally for our improvisational excursions

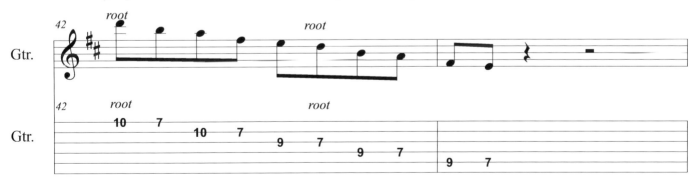

The following example uses the pentatonic scale but adds a couple of non-scale tones -- the F note in the first beat of the 3rd measure and the final run in the 4th bar use non scale tones for a cool sound.

Badlands

Dropped D tuning:
DADGBE

Pete Madsen

"Badlands" is another dropped-D composition that is centered around an A-shaped D minor chord. The opening sequence (first 4 bars) is mainly about using the 4th and 6th strings as drone notes and then at the end of the repeat on the 4th bar we chromatically walk into a partial A-shaped D minor chord. This section is surrounded by ascending and descending chromatic runs. We then play an E-shaped G7 chord, but again the low bass note has to be fretted two frets up from normal because of the 6th string being lowered. We descend from this chord down to an F, then an E and Eb that uses open strings. This section finishes off with an E-shaped Fmajor7th chord and repeats back to the beginning.

After the second pass through we end up at bar 16 where we employ a higher voiced version of the D minor we were playing in measures 5-9. This eight bar section uses a G-shape G chord with notes that descend on the 4th and 5th strings (measures 17 and 21); an E-shape A and G chords (measure 19) and the same E and Eb chords form the previous section. We then play one more pass through this eight bar section but with an improvisational aspect. I use the D minor measure to play licks based on minor pentatonic scales.

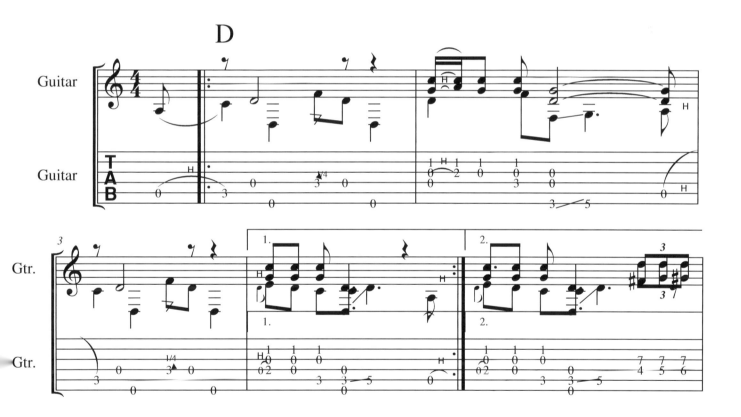

65

Stingy Brim

Dropped D Tuning:
DADGBE

Pete Madsen

Stingy Brim is another original tune that I had a lot of fun with. The opening A chord falls into a category which makes it hard to describe in CAGED terms. In essence its an A major chord with a #9 and a 6th thrown in. The A7 chord in measure 3 uses a C-shape and since it shares the same alternating bass notes as the first chord I think of it as an extension of that same shape. In measure 7 we work down the fretboard to play an E-shaped A7 chord. The D chord in measure 9 is a bit of a stretch, but it allows us to get some cool voicings via pull-offs and a descending bass line. The E chord in measure 17 is typical except that because we are in a dropped tuning we have to fret the low E note at the 2nd fret.

The pull-off sequence in measure 33-36 uses partial versions of an A-shape, C7-shape and D7 shape. The E → D sequence in measures 41-44 uses C-shapes with pull-offs.

We start a new section in measure 49, which uses descending lines and shapes under an alternating bass. The rest of these shapes should be familiar by now.

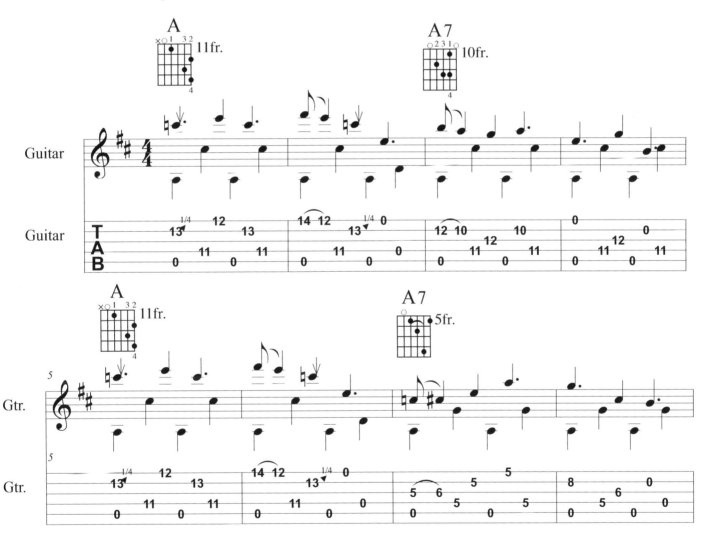

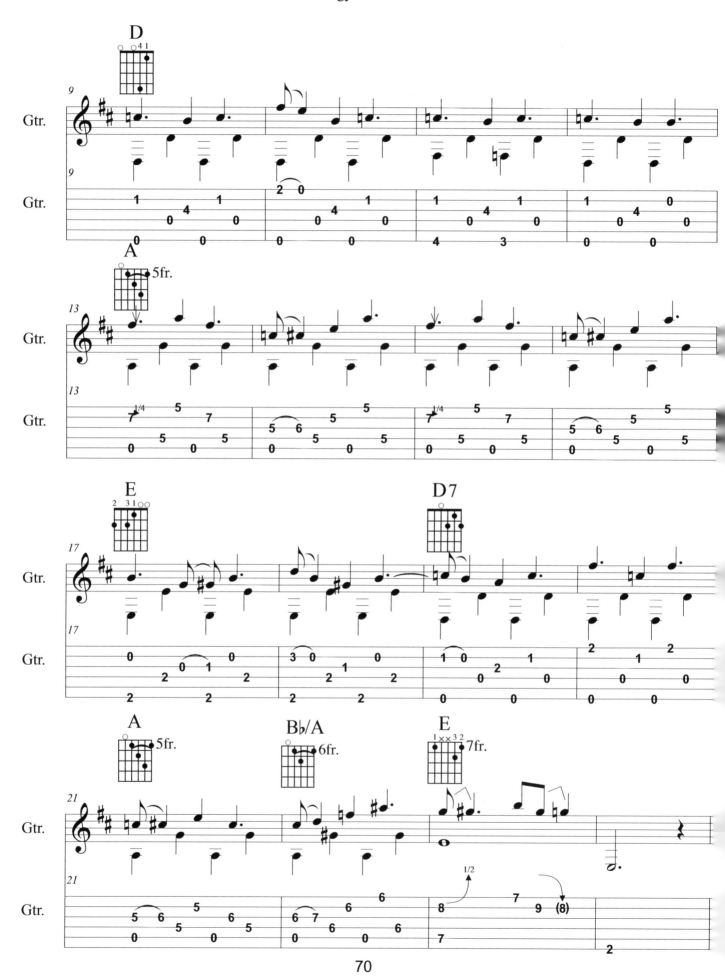

Stingy Brim

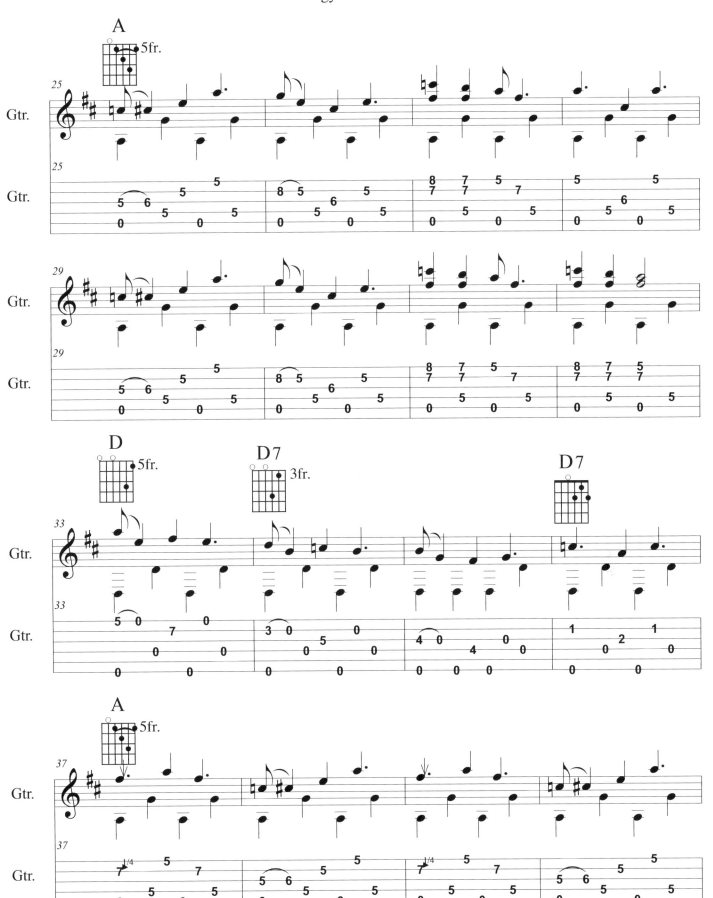

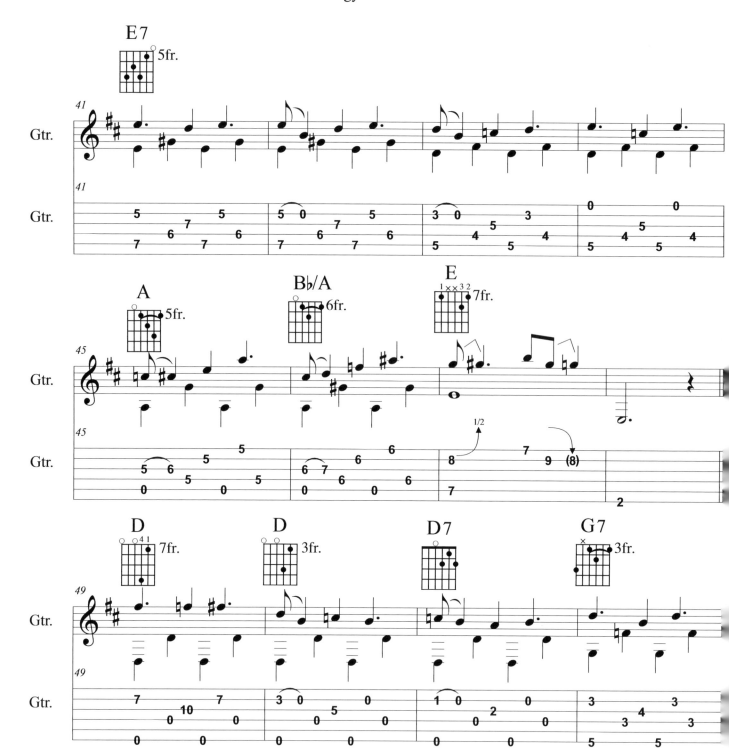

Stingy Brim

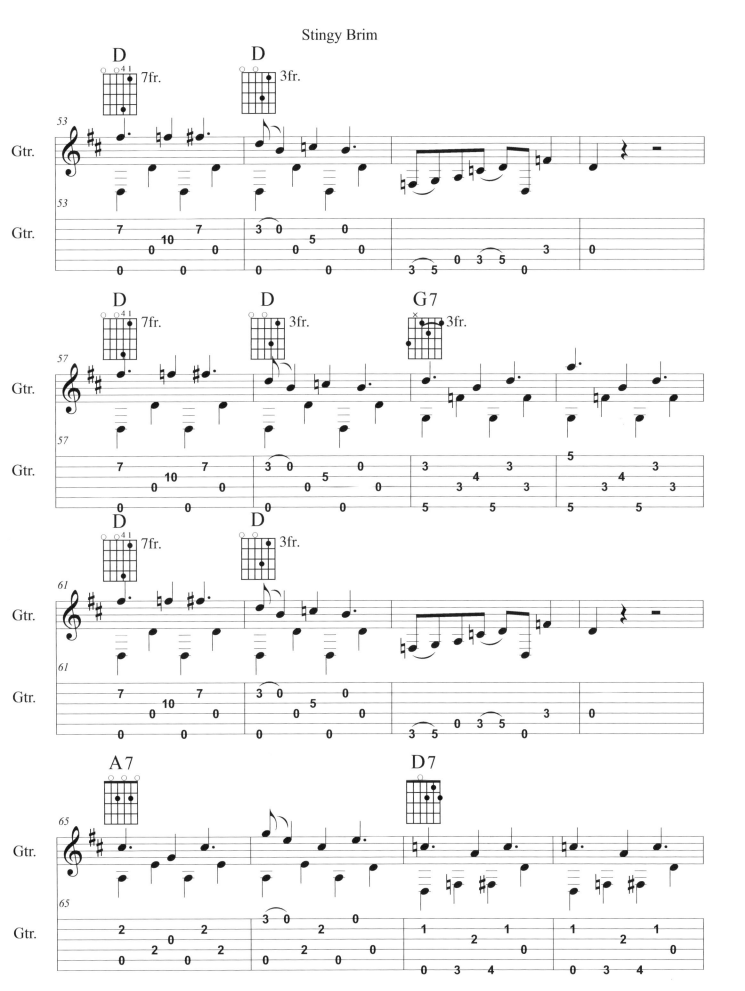

Stingy Brim

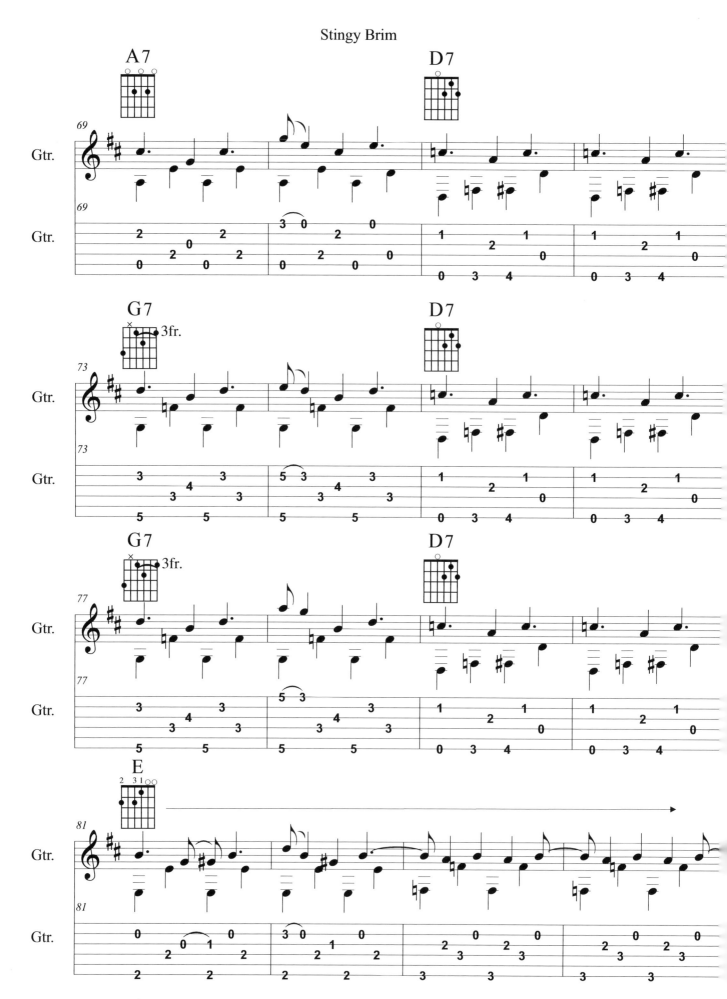

Stingy Brim

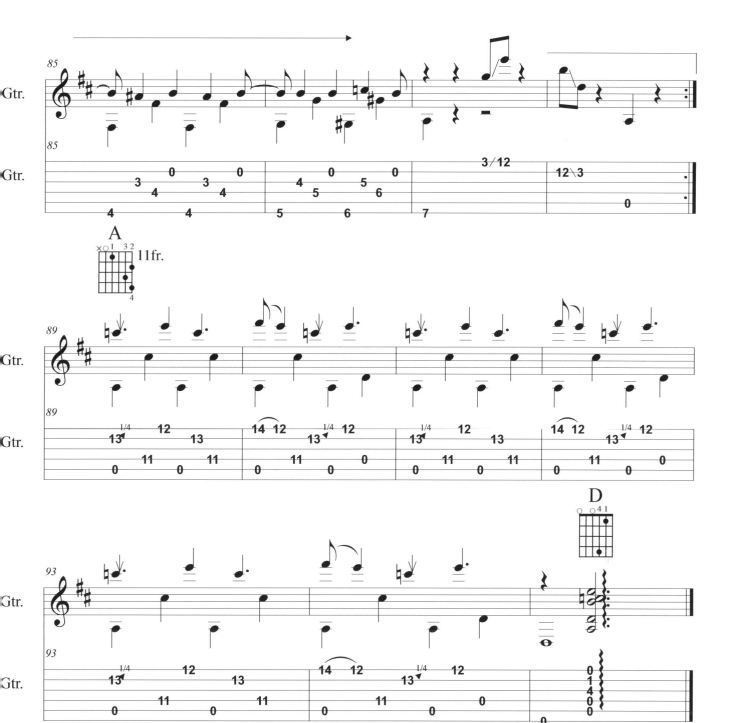

CHAPTER 4:
Advanced Songs

In this chapter we will learn:

- *Two longer/more complicated songs*

  - *Shuffle Rag*

  - *Pass the Jug*

Shuffle Rag

Broonzy

This is a Big Bill Broonzy song from late in his career, although there is a lot of an earlier composition called "Long Tall Mama" that is very similar. It's a twelve bar blues rag in C with myriad variations. All the variations with the exception of the third and 5th are pretty close to what Broonzy would play. The third variation is one I cooked up that uses a CAGED system idea - uses a partial G-shaped C chord and a partial C-shaped F chord. The 5th variation also uses CAGED chords; starting with a C-shaped C chord, moving to an A-shaped C chord, then to an E-shaped C chord and finally a D-shaped C7 chord. Watch out for the single string runs that are played towards the end of each variation. These can be tricky and must retain the swing groove. This song is a real show-stopper!

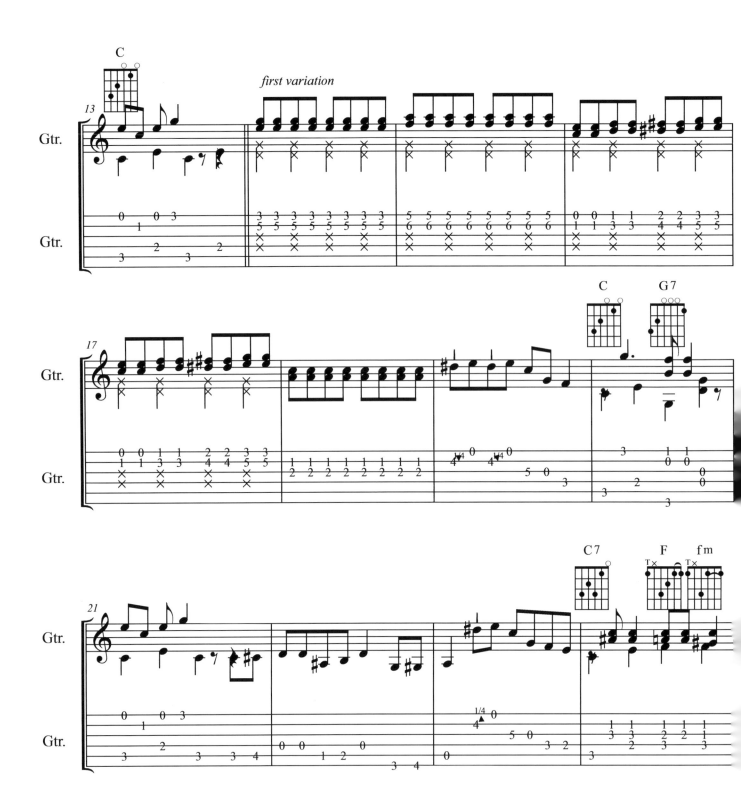

78

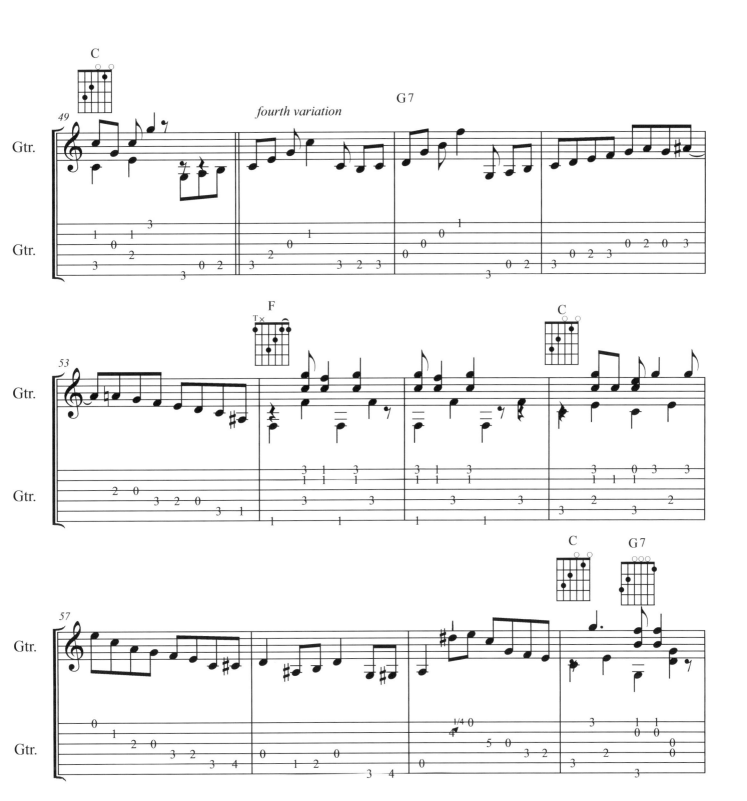

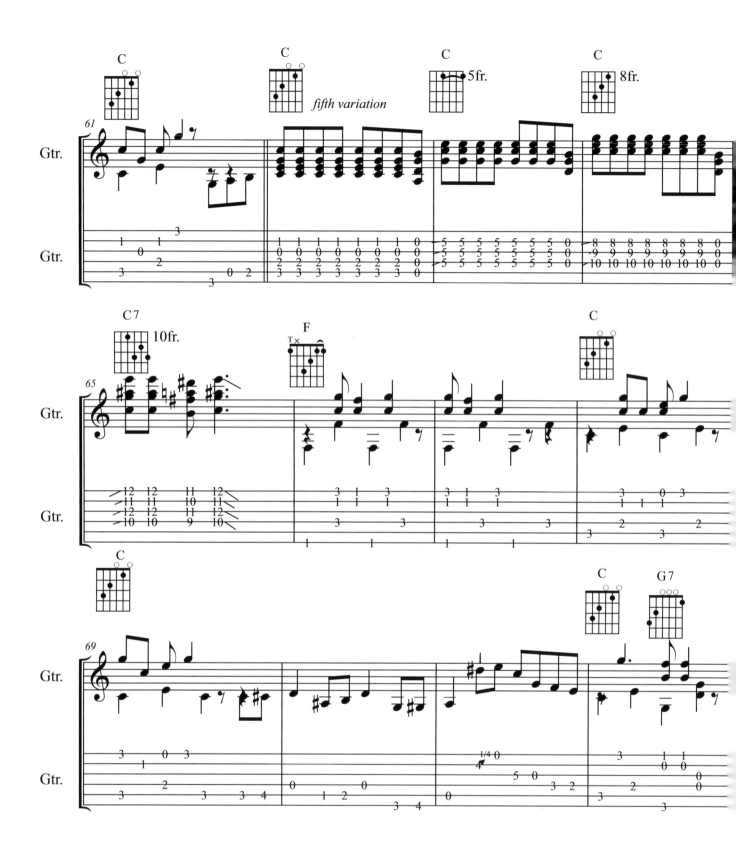

sixth variation

83

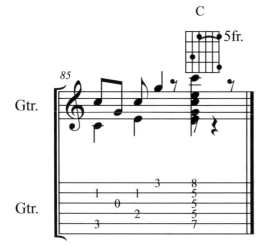

Pass the Jug

Okay, now to test our skills on a challenging tune called "Pass the Jug." The tune was written by pianist Frank Melrose (1907-1941), who was one of the leading figures in the Chicago blues and jazz scene of the 1920s and 30s. I heard a version of this tune played by New Orleans pianist, David Boeddinghaus on the compendium CD for the film "Crumb" and fell in love with its spirit and syncopations. Like most ragtime blues played on the piano this song was written in C, but I moved it to D to make it a little more "guitar-friendly."

The opening 32 bar A section moves mostly between B minor and G7. I use my thumb over the top of the neck to fret the 6th string on the G7 and F#7 chords. In measure 17 we slide up to an E-shaped B minor chord, which also uses the thumb over the neck.

At measure 33 we enter the B section, which is a series of 12 bars built around D/G/A chord changes. The first D chord is an abbreviated G-shape and then moves quickly to an abbreviated C-shaped G chord and then back to D. In measure 36 we use partial chords based on an A-shaped D and C-shaped D9. In bar 37, moving back to the IV chord, we use an E-shaped G7 and perform a double pull-off – notice that I keep the 4th string open, making this a little easier to fret.

In the next 12 bar sequence we use a series of partial chords to navigate between different voicings of D7. At the end of measure 44 we use a partial A-shaped D7 that "drifts" back down to a more basic d-shaped D7 chord –albeit with an F# in the bass. We can use similar partial chords to outline our G7 chord played in measures 49-50. *Note – we don't make the quick IV change in this verse.* When we come to the A/Bb chords we will play the commonly used G-shape.

The next verse uses a C-shaped D7 chord. I find this passage a little tricky to play because it involves some finger movement that can be a little "crampy." The chord starts out as a normal C7-shape, but then index finger moves into the 4th fret. In measure 58 we change to a D9 chord and "walk" the pinky to play the various melody notes. The G chord in this verse uses a walking bass line – bass line should be played with the index fretting. This sequays back to D7, using a variation on the C-shape that I borrowed from Big Bill Broonzy's "Saturday Night Rub."

The 4th verse in this section gives us a break by using conventional D7 and G7 chords and using some trills to make a statement. We punctuate this verse with a series of diminished chords.

The next verse, starting at measure 81, uses another walking bass line in which the thumb will fret not only 6th string but the 5th string as well. In measure 82 we perform another quick IV to G and then back to D7.

I find the 6th verse, starting at measure 93 the most challenging. We are playing the same walking bass as before but we are adding in more melody notes and this makes this a bit of a finger-buster. Again, for the D7 chord I will use my thumb to fret the 6th and 5th strings. The tricky part is that while your thumb and 3rd finger are moving around playing the bass, your index finger will be flicking on and off as part of the melody line – a real rubbing your head and patting your stomach kind of thing.

Pass the Jug

Melrose

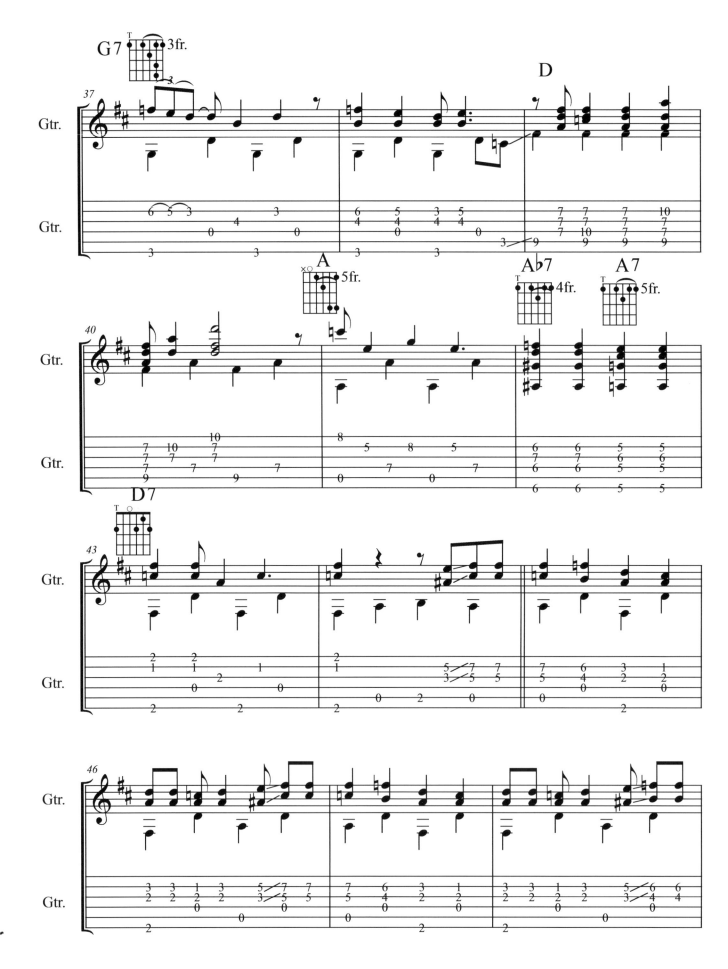

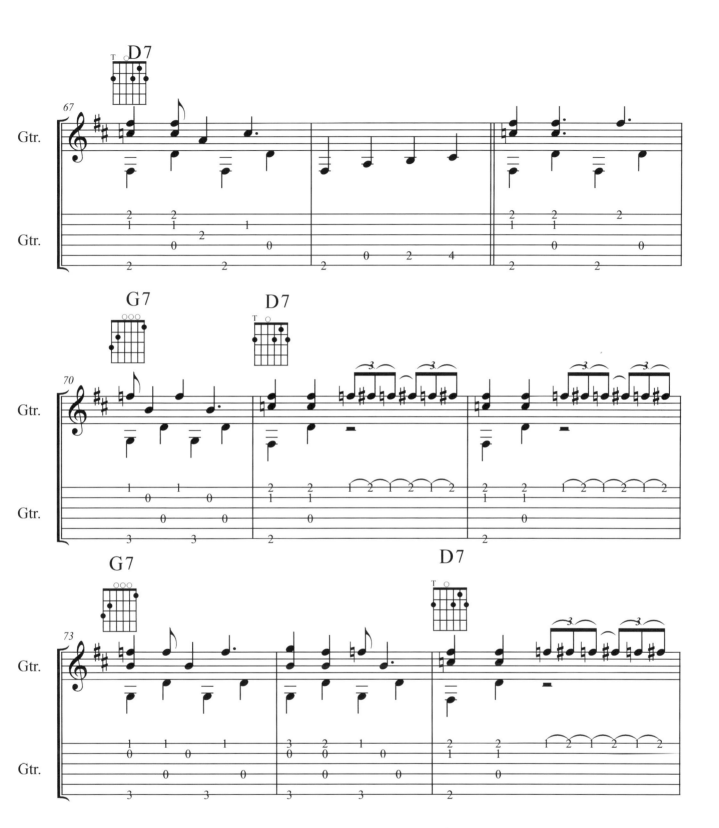

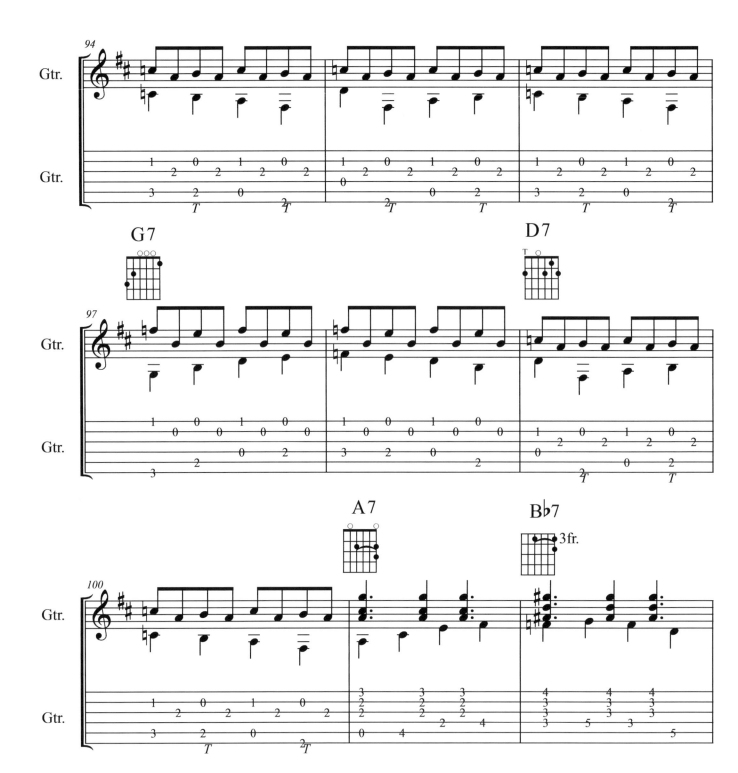

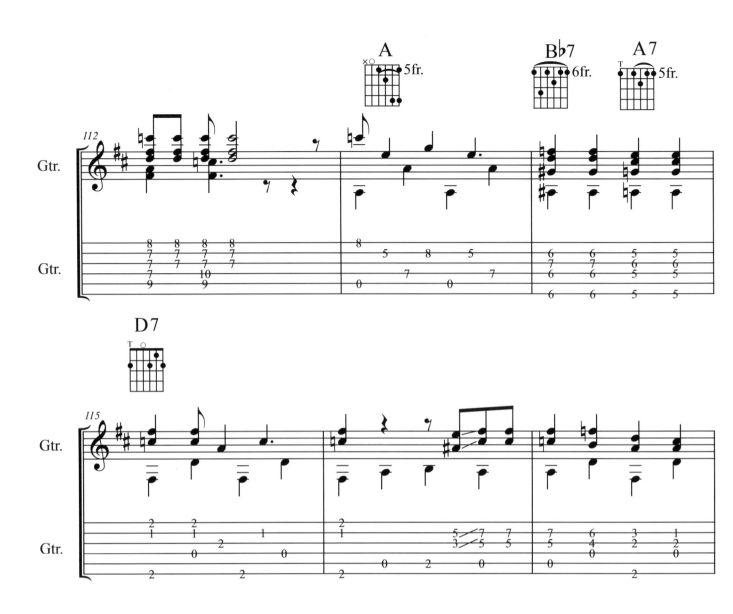

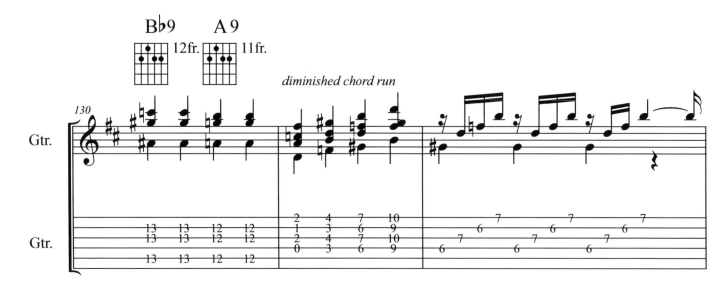

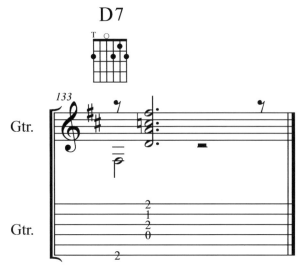

CHAPTER 5:
Scales, Riffs, Bass Runs and Combinations

In this chapter we will learn:

• *Pentatonic and Blues Scales in the keys of A, G and E*

• *riffs based on scales*

• *combine elements from scales and CAGED shapes to produce more cool phases.*

• *Bass runs in E for the song "Hey, Hey."*

Introduction to Chapter 5:
SCALES, RIFFS, BASS RUNS and COMBINATIONS

In this section we will add some components beyond the CAGED system to use for improvising. I'm sure that many of you are already familiar with pentatonic and blues scales, however I thought I should include them here because you may have only used them for soloing in an accompanied environment – playing with others. We can, of course, use these scales in our fingerstyle playing. I will focus on just a few keys in this section (E, A and G). The keys of E and A are more friendly to improvising because we can keep a constant monotonic (dead thumb) bass pattern using open strings.

In the beginning of this section I have given you some scales in the different keys we will be addressing. If you want more information on playing scales in ALL keys you can certainly find it on-line. But, I also feel that you can probably figure out other keys on your own simply by transferring the positions I have given you.

We can also add bass runs for flavor or as a way to navigate between the chord changes.

Finally, we can combine ideas from CAGED, scales and riffs and create some cool new verses.

A Minor Pentatonic scales

Licks are often derived form scales. We will be using 5 positions of minor pentatonic scales to play lick and riffs. You should try to memorize the following scales

1st position

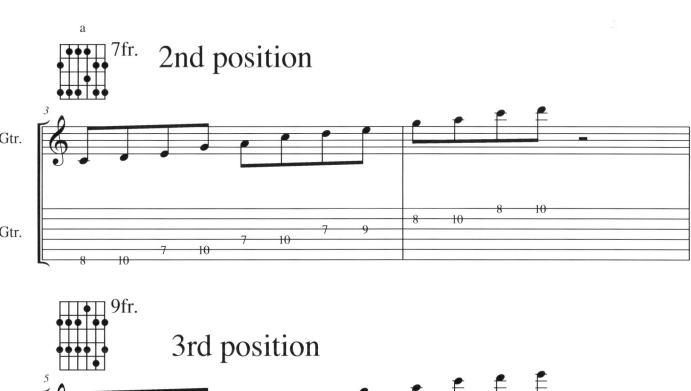

2nd position

3rd position

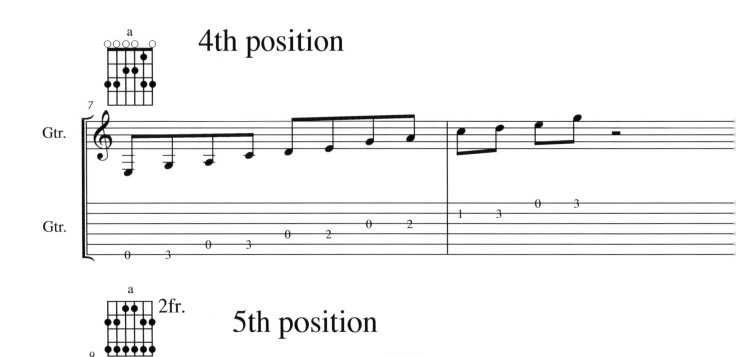

4th position

5th position

G Minor Pentatonic

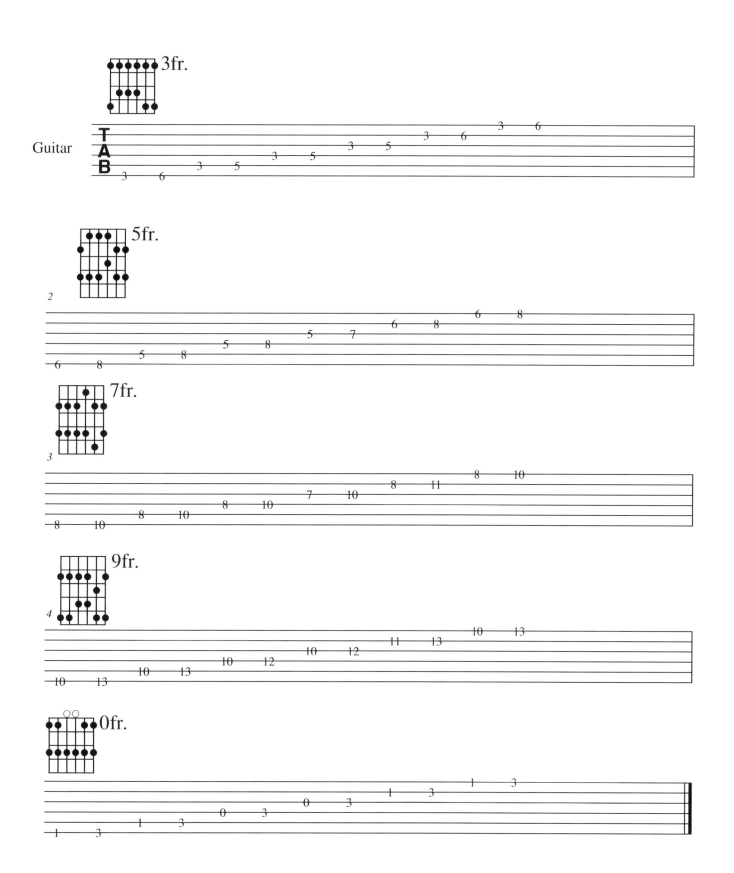

G Blues scales

The Blues scale can be thought of as a modified minor pentatonic scale. Instead of five notes we have six. The minor pentatonic is contructed of: 1 (root) 3b (flatted third), 4th, 5th and 7b (flatted). The Blues scale adds a flatted 5th. In the diagrams below the flatted 5th is signified with an open circle (*except where note

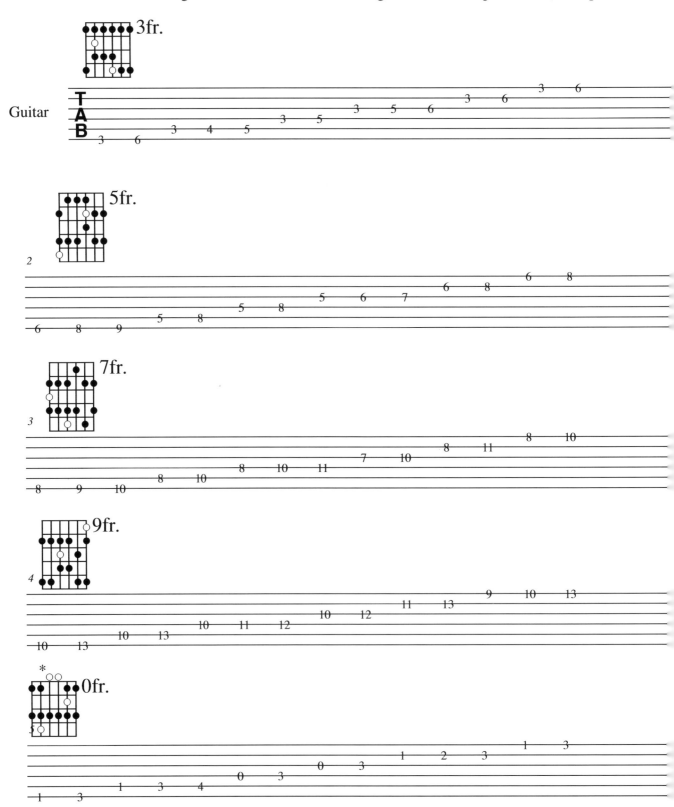

106

E minor pentatonic scales

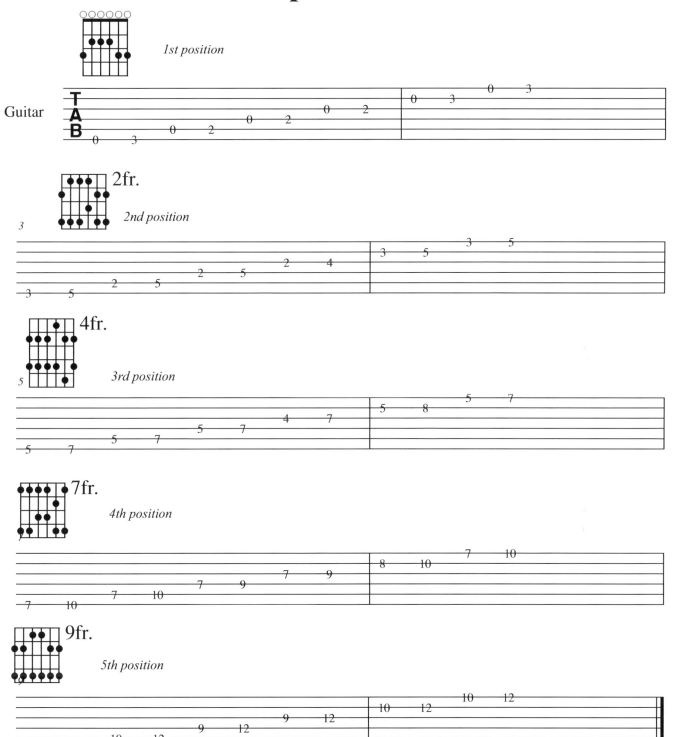

E Blues Scales

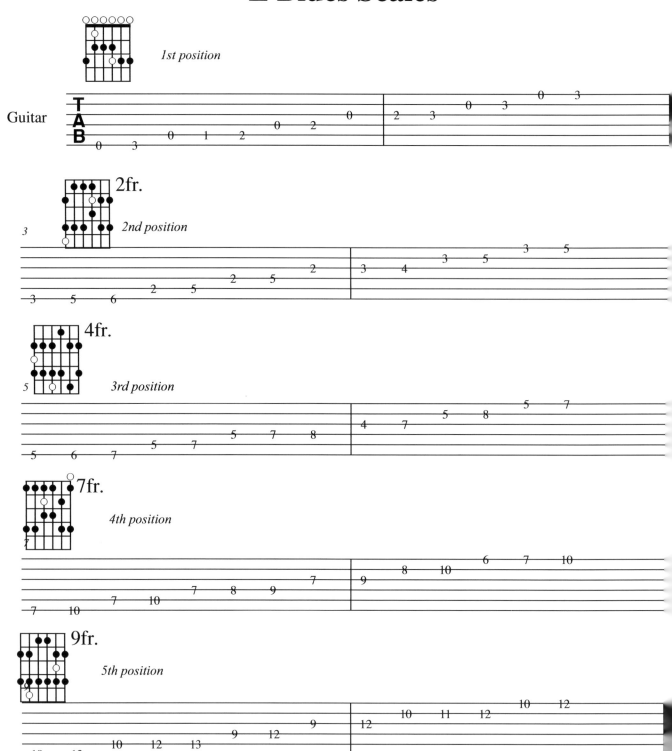

Monotonic CAGED Improv 1

This 12 bar blues in G will have us combing 3 elements: 1) a monotonic (dead thumb) bass pattern, 2) CAGED chord shapes and 3) scale tones. For all versions of the G chord I use my thumb to cover the 6th string. In the first 12 bar I keep a steady G bass on the 6th string and work various pentatonic and chromatic scale tones underneath. You can think of these notes as extension of an E-shape G7 chord.

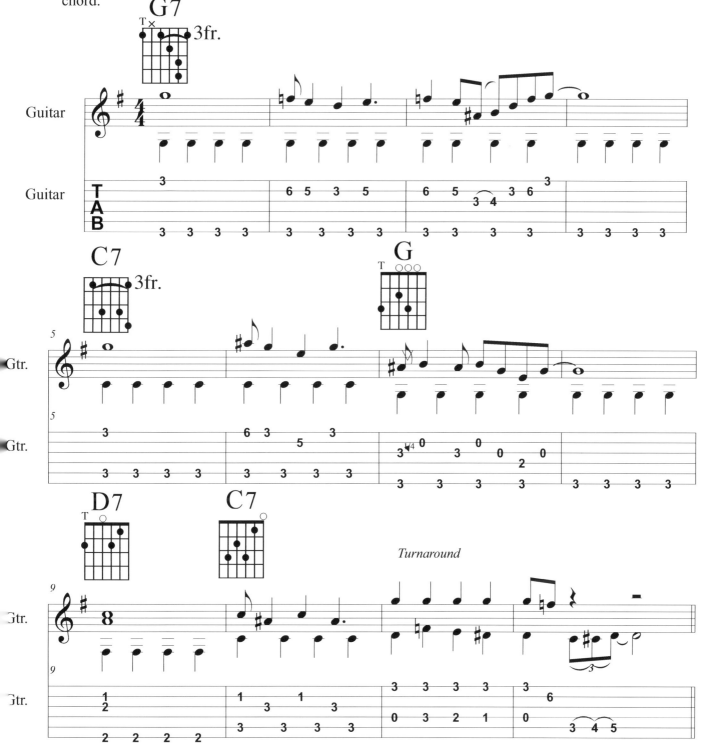

Blending CAGED ideas with Blues scales

A lot of early fingerpicked blues use an alternating bass (played between 2 or more strings), but many other grooves employ a single string or "dead" thumb bass. In this lesson we will work through a 12 bar blues in E with a single string bass. We will also play a 12 bar variation on that theme. The groove is simple, but requires keeping that steady bass which can be more difficult than it at first seems.

In the first verse we will stick to primarily E Blues scales notes in the treble voice. In the second verse we will incorporate CAGED ideas that will flesh-out the harmony.

If you can count to 4 and tap your foot you can play blues. Yes, this is true, but there is so much more to it! The bass pattern that we play with our thumb is steady and percussive. What I mean by "percussive" is that the bass notes are often muted and sound less like actual notes and more like someone beating a drum: a low throbbing, audible drum. This underlies everything else and can get lost in the shuffle – no pun intended! The trick, then, is to make the treble notes sound like they have an entirely different voice. Part of this is simply rhythmic: where is the treble played in relation to the bass. But part of it – the part that is difficult to articulate – is feel. Yes, you can look at the TAB, but more importantly, listen to the music.

PRACTICE TIP: Listen, Listen, Listen. I can't emphasize this enough. After fifteen years of teaching I still need to remind students that one of the most important parts of their practice is "informal" listening, i.e. listening for pleasure. As we listen our conscious and unconscious mind form connections. Struggling through a difficult passage of TAB is only as much fun as your ear dictates.

Another aspect to getting the feel correct is repetition. Playing the same thing over and over again can be tedious, but in the process of repeating these phrases your appendages learn how to make things sound good! The process goes something like this:
1) Learn the phrase(s)
2) Repeat
3) Create a feel
4) Sound good!

In the beginning of "Big Dog Blues" we play very sparsely; this gives us the opportunity to set the groove. By the third measure we are ready for something a little more busy and thus the riff that sounds a little like "Susie-Q" – the riff created many decades ago by James Burton.
When we shift to the A chord in measure 5 we play the 5th string as our bass note with a short simple series of notes played on the 3rd and 2nd strings. When we come back to the E chord we repeat the "Susie-Q" riff. We then play a quick B7 and finish off the first 12 bar with the "Q" riff.

In the second 12 bar we move up the fretboard to play an E minor triad in between the 7thg 9th frets (see fret graph in TAB). This is an A minor shape. I think this riff sounds extra cool! So cool, I play it again. Then, when we move to the A chord, which can be thought of as a Dg shape A7.

When we get to the B chord in the 4th to last measure I shift the melodic emphasis to the bass. This requires that you move your index and middle fingers down to the 5th and 4th strings respectively to fingerpick those strings. Both the A and B chords in this section are based out of E shapes.

Bad Dog Blues

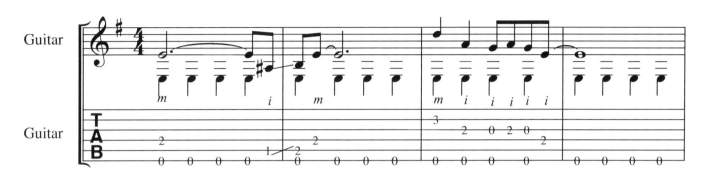

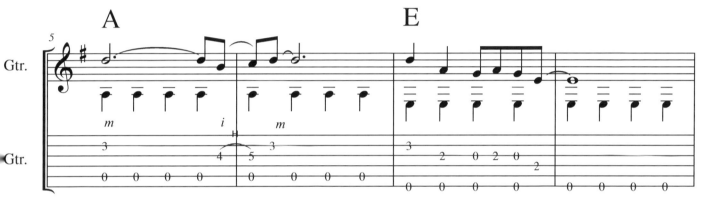

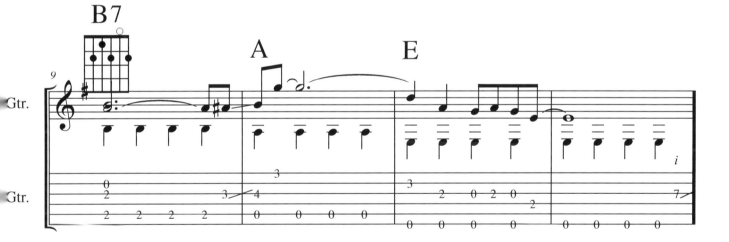

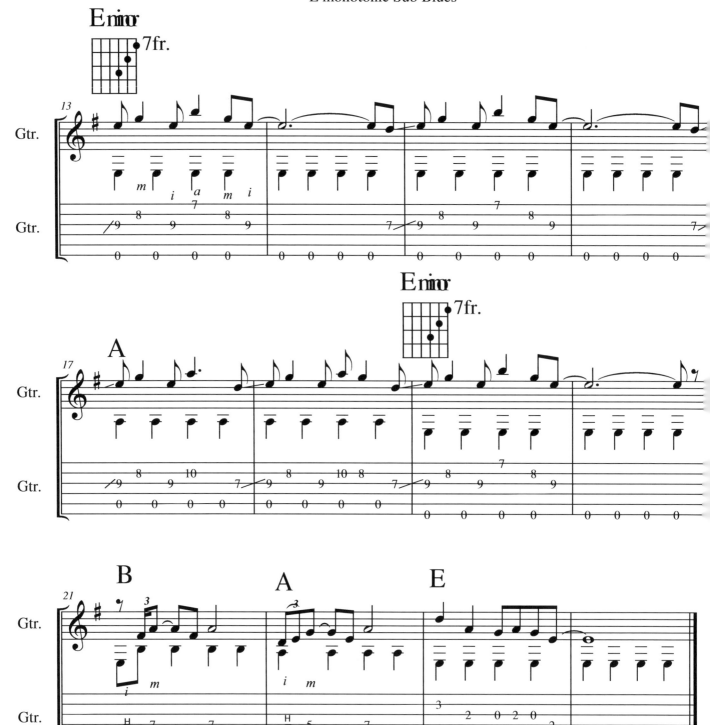

E minor Improvisation #1

In some of the early delta-style blues there were no chord changes. Players like Skip James and Charlie Patton would play single chord grooves. In the key of E we can navigate the entire fretboard while keeping a steady bass groove on the 6th string. This can create a hypnotic effect as we construct a piece of music out of what appears to be nothing.

As an experiment I decided to just play and record myself, with no intent other than to create a solid groove and to work the entire fretboard. This is what I came up with. You will notice that I tend to think and play in 4 bar phrases. Hmmm. I guess this is a natural enough component of my many years of playing.

I decided that I would record, then transcribe and analyze after the fact so here we go:

The first four bars are centered around a partial E7 and a first position E minor pentatonic scale. The next four bar segment works the 4th position E minor pentatonic, as does the 3rd four bar section. The section starting at measure 13 uses a pedal tone (E) that I combine with a chromatic run on the second string. In the section starting at measure 17 I start out in a 5th position E minor pentatonic scale and work my way down to a third position pentatonic. Measure 21-28 use a 4th position pentatonic and work down to a first position.

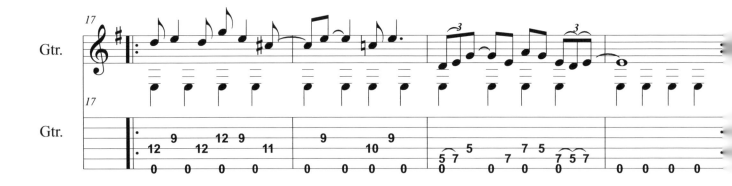

Improv 12 bar in A

This was another experiment. I decided to play a 12 bar blues in the key of A, keeping a steady monotonic bass pattern. This meant I was using A, D and E chords. Again, I had no idea what I was going to play – and that lead to some redundancy. I ended up playing five different verses. There are a lot of similar riffs and partial chords here; but in each 12 bar there is a slightly different emphasis. For instance, I start off with single string licks in the first verse, but then gradually incorporate more double-stops.

In the first verse I start off with a lick that uses the flat five (Eb), and then return to that note over the IV chord (D). Measures 7-11 are all about double-stops/partial chords

In the beginning of the second verse I arpeggiate a D-shape A7 chord, moving the emphasis to a slightly higher register – I believe this is an unconscious decision based on listening to and playing songs like Robert Johnson's "Kind Hearted Woman." In measures 14-16 I transition from this chord through some double-stops that lead me in to playing a pentatonic lick, which leads me right back to the D7 chord I played from the previous verse – I told you there was some redundancies. Part of this is habit and being in a location on the neck with a chord change coming up and having to make a quick decision. Measure 23-24 are a classic Robert Johnson turnaround, of which there will be a couple of other versions later on.

In the third verse, because I was close to the nut, I tried working some of the 5th position pentatonic scale (See scales at the beginning of the chapter). These licks require a bit of a finger stretch, but don't let that stop you; you can often get some really cool licks by playing adjacent strings with finger stretches. I should point out that in measure 33 the E chord is being fretted as an C7 shape, as is the subsequent D chord, but with a higher voicing.

For me the fourth verse was a "time killer." I really didn't bring anything new to the mix. Although I added double-stops to the D chord, which was played in the first verse.

In the fifth verse I brought in another higher voiced A7 chord – a C-shape played between the 10-12th frets. After a couple of bars of that I moved into a classic lick played out of a 4th position pentatonic that uses the second string bent up a half step. Since I'm that high up on the neck I use an E-shape barre at the 10th fret for my D chord. Back at A, I move from my double-stop lick into a chord voicing that has a flat 7, 9th and suspended 4th in it. I'm not sure what its called, but it sounds good!

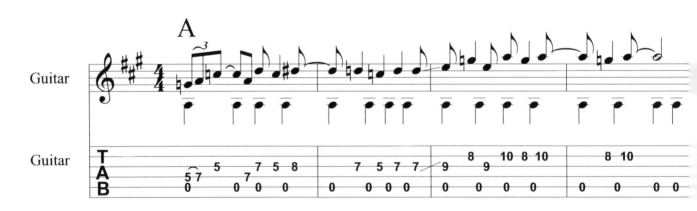

Improv 12 bar in A

119

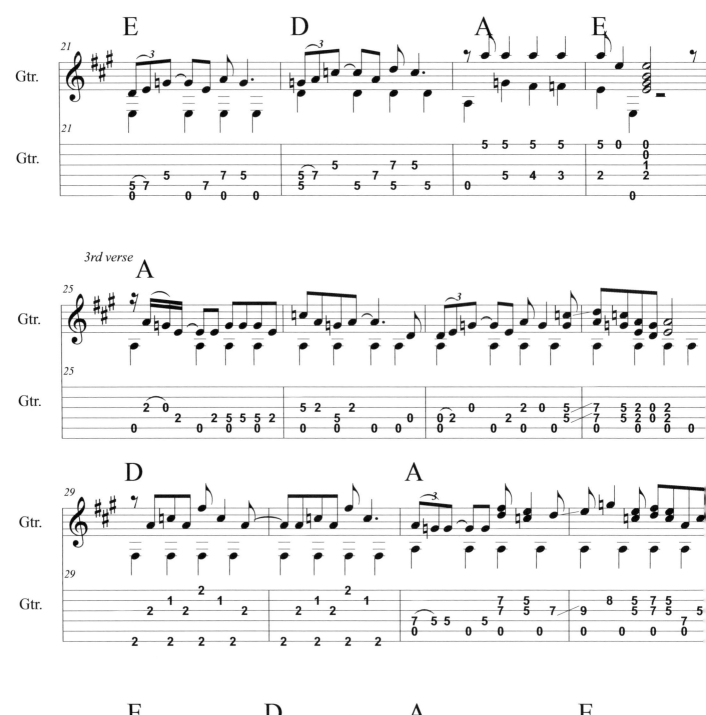

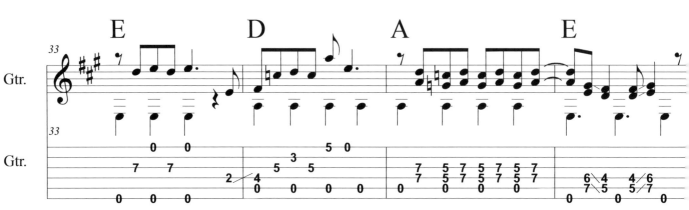

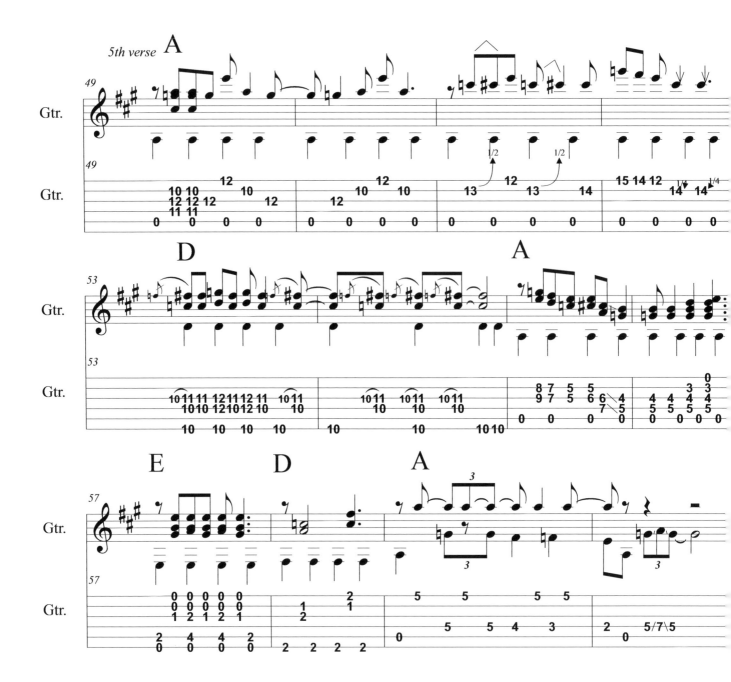

Hey, hey
improvisation w/bass

Bill Broonzy

Big Bill Broonnzy is perhaps my favorite early blues guitarist. The syncopation and rhythmic drive of his guitar playing is unparalleled. His early recordings, with fellow guitarist Frank Brasswell, were good-time party tunes. "Hey, Hey," is one of his later recordings - laid down in the 1950s. Unlike "Pig Meat Strut," another blues in the key of E, Hey, Hey" uses a single string bass (called "monotonic") rather than an alternating bass pattern.

"Hey, Hey" is deceptively simple. At first look you might feel you can cruise right through it, but the syncopation can be a little difficult.

In the second verse I have added some bass runs which require you to fret the chords a little differently. We use the 2nd, 3rd and 4th fingers to fret the D-shaped E7 chord, which allows us to use the 1st and 4th fingers to play the bass run in measure 14. Our previous fingering for A-A7 works for the bass run we play in measure 18. The B chord in measure 21 starts out as an A-shape, but quickly morphs into more of a G-shape, as we have to navigate up the 6th fret on the 5th string.

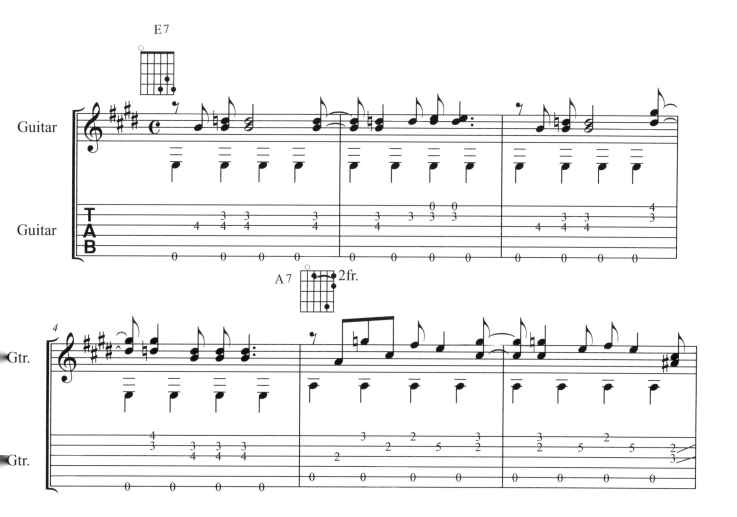

TAB Ex

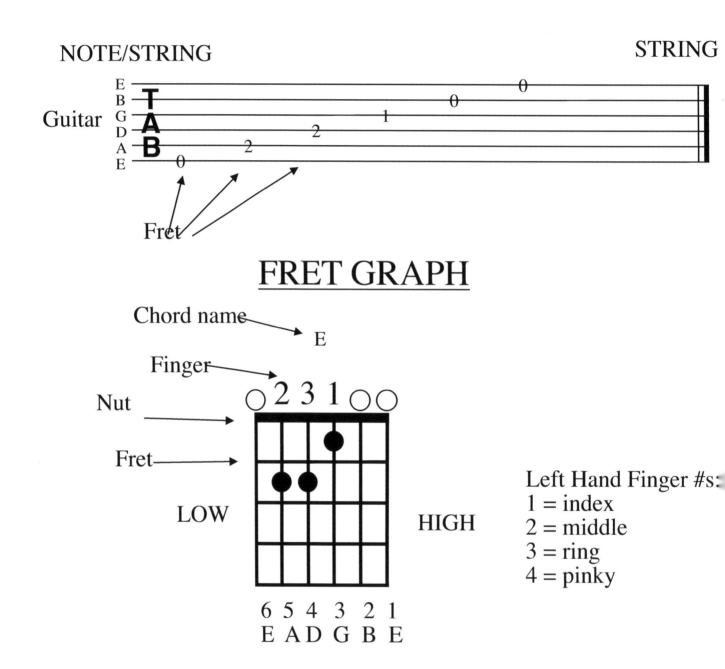

NOTE/STRING

STRING

Guitar

Fret

FRET GRAPH

Chord name → E

Finger

Nut

Fret

LOW   HIGH

6 5 4 3 2 1
E A D G B E

Left Hand Finger #s:
1 = index
2 = middle
3 = ring
4 = pinky

The two illustrations above represent a measue of TAB and a FRET GRAPH. TAB is musical notation specifically for the guitar. Each line represents a string, from 1 (Hi E) to 6 (low E). The numbers represented on each line tell you which FRET to play. The FRET GRAPH is like a picture of the guitar fretboard. In this example is telling you where to put your fingers to make an E chord

126

TAB legend

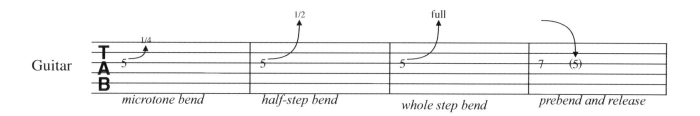

Guitar

microtone bend half-step bend whole step bend prebend and release

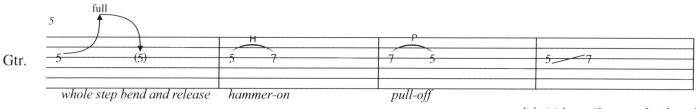

Gtr.

whole step bend and release hammer-on pull-off

slide (either w/finger or bottleneck)

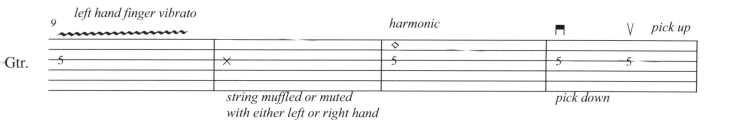

Gtr.

left hand finger vibrato *harmonic* *pick up*

string muffled or muted *pick down*
with either left or right hand

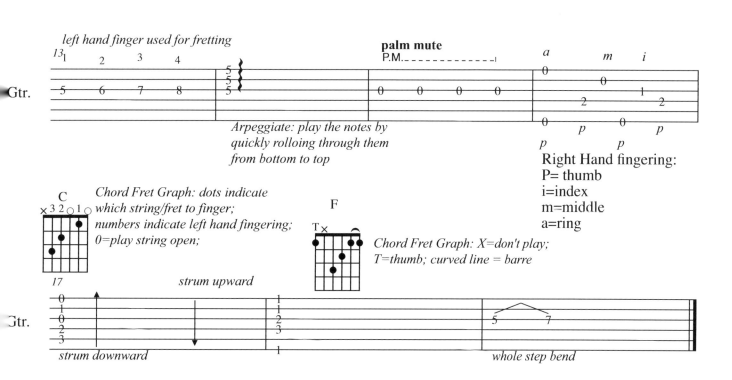

Gtr.

left hand finger used for fretting **palm mute**

Arpeggiate: play the notes by
quickly rolloing through them
from bottom to top

Right Hand fingering:
P= thumb
i=index
m=middle
a=ring

C

Chord Fret Graph: dots indicate
which string/fret to finger;
numbers indicate left hand fingering;
0=play string open;

F

Chord Fret Graph: X=don't play;
T=thumb; curved line = barre

Gtr.

strum upward

strum downward *whole step bend*

Printed in Great Britain
by Amazon

36281834R00073